EAST
OF MALAGA

ESSENTIAL GUIDE
TO THE AXARQUÍA AND
COSTA TROPICAL

David Baird

SANTANA BOOKS

East of Málaga
Published by Ediciones Santana SL
Apartado 41
26950 Mijas-Pueblo (Málaga)
Spain

Tel: (0034) 952 48 58 38
Fax: (0034) 952 48 53 67
E-Mail: info@santanabooks.com

Copyright©2007 David Baird
All photos by David Baird
Designed by Chris Fajardo
Map of the Axarquía courtesy of APTA
(Asociación para la Promoción Turística de la
Axarquía)

Printed in Spain by Grafisur.

ISBN: 978-84-89954-63-2
Depósito Legal: CA - 594-07

CONTENTS

Axarquia village street

INTRODUCTION

ABOUT 90 years ago an English traveller — eager to reach the Mediterranean coast — came walking from Granada across stubbled, dusty plains. Confronted by a dramatic range of mountains, he climbed for hour after hour until he reached the last crest just as the sun dipped towards the horizon.

Looking down, he noted later: "I could pick out the villages of the Axarquía far below me, the smoke rising above them in short columns and then ending. From this height they looked like splashes of white paint dropped on to a surge of pale red hills that ran off the grey rock mountain like fingers and fell in successive cones and waves and rounded protuberances to the sea. Beyond that, very far off, floating on the haze, lay the coastline of Africa."

Much has changed since Gerald Brenan, later to become famous for his writings on Spain, stumbled across this corner of Málaga province. But it's still possible to wonder at the same view, for the region retains a magical quality.

Covering 988 square kilometres and embracing 31 municipalities with a population of around 130,000, the Axarquía resembles a vast amphitheatre. It and the 80-kilometre stretch of Granada's aptly named Costa Tropical are shielded from the bitter blasts from the north by a jagged range of mountains. The result: one of the mildest climates in Europe, with around 3,000 hours of sunshine every year. While traditional crops, grapes, olives, almonds, grow on the upper slopes, tropical fruits flourish towards the coast.

Escapists, artists, writers, drop-outs have long known about the Axarquía (from the Arabic *sharquiyya*, meaning the eastern zone). But mass tourism, along with its worst excesses, is a recent arrival in this corner of Málaga province. The traffic went mainly west towards Gibraltar, to Torremolinos, Fuengirola and Marbella.

Poor communications meant the Costa del Sol Oriental — running from the provincial capital into Granada province — was largely bypassed by travellers. Most visitors to southern Spain took more direct inland routes to Granada rather than tackle the tortuous coastal highway towards Almería.

No longer. For good or ill, the coast east of Málaga has taken off. Even the remotest, most slumbersome of the whitewashed villages that dot the hills have felt the impact of change. Improved communications have converted the Axarquía and the Costa Tropical into popular tourist destinations.

Large numbers of north Europeans have settled along the coast and the sleepy, whitewashed villages, olive groves, vineyards and stark sierras are attracting more and more visitors inland, thanks to the growth of rural tourism.

The construction frenzy that has raged along Spain's Mediterranean coast in the early years of the new millenium has not left the Axarquía and Costa Tropical untouched. Ancient vines and olive groves have been uprooted to make way for urbanisations and villas, some in open defiance of planning legislation. A Ley de Costas prohibits development within 100 metres of the sea, but innumerable ways have been found to get around it.

While concrete advances relentlessly across a landscape that barely changed during centuries, there is a positive side: villages that were desperately poor until recently are prospering and facilities have greatly improved.

Today explorers of this region will find delightful small hotels and good-quality restaurants as well as facilities for all manner of outdoor activities, from mountain biking to hiking, scuba-diving to canyoning.

They will also find what Laurie Lee described in *A Rose for Winter* after

Maroma snow

visiting the Costa Tropical (long before that name was invented):
"The warmth of the sun fell on us like a treasure, and the daylight moved over the sea in great, slow transpositions of colour, dying each night in purple dusks. The cliffs and mountains soaked up the sunsets like red sponges and the distant ragged edge of the sierras shone blue as a blunted saw."

Magical imagery. But you don't have to be a poet like Lee to be moved to lyrical heights by the natural wonders of the region east of Málaga.

Bandolero plaque

HISTORY'S LONG FOOTPRINT

IN 1965, John Wilkins, formerly of the Royal Canadian Air Force, and his wife found the perfect location for their retirement: a bare hilltop between Nerja and Frigiliana. There they set about building a comfortable home — and discovered a treasure trove.

The builders came across a number of large ceramic urns, lodged in rock cavities. Inside were what looked like ashes. Wilkins promptly informed the authorities and excited archeologists descended on El Cerrillo de las Sombras.

At first they were convinced it was an important Phoenician burial ground. Later research, however, suggests the remains belong to Iberian settlers, culturally part of the fabled kingdom of Tartessus, which flourished from around 1,000 BC. Today those old pots, along with bones, brooches, needles and similar artefacts, are prized items in Frigiliana's Casa de la Cultura.

Wherever you dig in the Axarquía or along the Costa Tropical, the odds are you'll unearth some signs of early settlements or burial grounds. Some discoveries are almost certainly covered up for fear that construction work will be halted to allow lengthy investigations.

History cannot be ignored here for Iberians, Phoenicians, Greeks, Carthaginians, Romans, Arabs, Berbers have all left their imprints. Nobody can know how many caves - a useful shelter in pre-history for hunter-gatherers - await discovery in the territory's karstic limestone ranges .

In 1959 a spectacular complex came to light at Nerja, discovered by adventurous local youngsters. The vast underground chambers had been inhabited from 15,000 or more years ago until comparatively recent times, i.e. until a little before the birth of Christ.

Paleolithic (earlier than 10,000 BC) and Neolithic man (10,000-2,500 BC) left a mark in many locations, including cave paintings, tombs, ceramics, knives and other artefacts. The Cerro de la Corona dolmen at Totalán goes back about 2,500 years. In Granada province, a Neolithic necropolis exists at Los Castillejos, near Lentegí, and important vestiges of

Neolithic man were discovered in the Cueva de los Murciélagos (Bat Cave) near Albuñol.

Around 800 BC Phoenician traders established settlements at Cádiz, Málaga and Sexi (Almuñécar), where they set up a fish-curing centre. An important necropolis known as Laurita was found in 1962 on Almuñécar's Cerro de San Cristóbal. Alabaster urns were unearthed bearing hieroglyphics relating to 900BC Pharaohs and other finds included painted ostrich eggs. Excavations at another Almuñécar necropolis, Puente de Noy, have turned up 200 tombs. Phoenician amphoras and jewellery were found too at the Trayamar necropolis at Algarrobo (Málaga).

Later came the Carthaginians. They were crushed, in the Punic wars, by the Romans, who formed the province of Baetica in southern Spain. The Romans built enduring monuments along the coast (a revolutionary new technique employed volcanic sand called *pozzolana* to create water-resistant concrete).

Perhaps their most outstanding legacy is Almuñécar's aqueduct, in use for 2,000 years. The longest existing stretch, at Torrecuevas, runs for 130 metres. The town archeological museum is housed in a Roman vault known as the Cueva de Siete Palacios and the pits of a fish-salting factory are on view at the town's Majuelo Park. A similar factory, producing the prize export of *garum* sauce, existed at Caviclum, near the lighthouse at Torrox. There too are the remains of a Roman villa, a necropolis, ceramic ovens and baths.

Made from fish guts and liver, sometimes mixed with wine or oil, garum was either a foul-smelling dog's dinner or a gourmet's delight, depending on one's tastes. It was usually served as an aperitif, but it was also said to have remarkable medicinal properties, useful in cases of anemia.

Some researchers claim that Marco Craso, an illustrious Roman, took refuge for several months in one of the caverns of the Cueva del Tesoro at La Caleta, near Rincón. In this cave — unusual in that it was formed by marine erosion — animals were apparently sacrificed before a shrine dedicated to the Mediterranean lunar goddess Noctiluca.

At Valle Niza, near Vélez-Málaga, Phoenicians, Romans and Moors quarried stone to use in their buildings. The quarry was abandoned but reopened in the 18th-century when the stone was used in the construction of Málaga cathedral. Now Vélez offers guided visits to a Museo de la Piedra at the quarry. A centuries-old chapel has been restored at the site where a thousand or so years ago a Christian convent existed.

By the second and third centuries after Christ Christian communities existed throughout the peninsula. In 313 the Council of Iliberri (Granada), attended by 19 bishops and 24 presbyters, decreed that priests should be celibate.

INVASION FROM AFRICA

The Romans gave way to invaders from the north, Germanic tribes such as the Visigoths and Vandals. Although they held sway for some centuries, you will find few physical signs of their presence.

But the Vandals did give Vandalusia its name. The next invaders converted that to al-Andalus. They were the tribes from Africa, who first set foot at Gibraltar in 711 and soon dominated much of the peninsula.

The areas now known as Málaga and Granada provinces were to remain under Moorish rule for seven centuries — longer than any other part of Spain — and this left an indelible mark, in the character of the people, in the architecture and in the way of life (See Legacy of the Moors).

For two-and-a-half centuries the Nasrid dynasty of Granada ruled this southern corner of the peninsula, reaching its greatest splendour under Mohammed V in the 14th-century, when the magnificent Alhambra palace was constructed.

Morisco rebellion in Cómpeta

PIRATES ON THE COAST

Piracy was a constant threat in past centuries all along the Mediterranean coast. Communities lived in fear for at any moment the jackals of the seas could sweep in to rape, pillage and kidnap.

Small wonder that many settlements grew up on defensible hilltops set back from the coast. Even Vikings are said to have sailed into the Mediterranean to plunder, explaining perhaps the number of blond persons found in parts of Spain.

Romans built a series of towers along the coast where watch could be kept for likely attackers. The Moors improved and extended them, particularly Mohammed II, the 13th-century ruler of the Nasrid kingdom of Granada. When danger appeared over the horizon, the alarm went up via fires at night and smoke signals in daytime so that inhabitants could quickly retreat to safe refuges.

After the Reconquest, attacks by Turkish corsairs and pirates based on the Barbary Coast (present-day Algeria) persuaded the Christian rulers to reinforce this line of defence.

Miguel de Cervantes knew only too well the perils posed by pirates. He and his brother Rodrigo, sailing home from battling the Ottoman empire, were seized by corsairs and taken off to Algiers as slaves. Five years were to pass before a ransom was paid and he returned to his native land (popular belief says he stepped ashore at Mezquitilla).

Later the towers came in useful to watch for such traditional enemies as the English, the Portuguese and the French.

You will encounter these ancient structures all along the Málaga and Granada coasts. Usually on prominent headlands, some are on the point of collapse, others have been restored and one or two converted into homes.

They are known as *torres vigía* or *atalayas* and sometimes they are referred to as *torres almenares* — an *almenar* is a beacon. They recall the time when the cry "¡Hay moros en la costa!" was enough to send whole communities rushing for the hills.

CHRISTIAN SPAIN

In the late 15th-century the armies of the Christian Monarchs, Isabel and Fernando, laid siege to the last holdouts of the Moors. Málaga and Vélez-Málaga fell in 1487 and with them all the small villages of the Axarquía. In 1489 it was the turn of Almuñécar and surrounding settlements and in 1492 Granada itself was conquered.

Many of the Moorish inhabitants fled to the Alpujarras, the remote hills and valleys of the south-facing slopes of the Sierra Nevada. Others lived on in the hills of the Axarquía. Theoretically the Moors were allowed to retain their own customs as long they converted to Christianity, converts being known as Moriscos. As the Inquisition tightened its grip, however, their traditional ways, even their music and habit of taking frequent baths, were condemned as heretical.

In 1567 the Moriscos were given three years to abandon their customs, language and style of dress and to assume Christian

King Fernando

Queen Isabel la Católica

names. The move inflamed the Moriscos and in December, 1568, they crowned a new king in the Alpujarras, Aben Humeya.

One of his aides sneaked into Granada's Albaicín district and instigated rebellion, which swiftly spread from the Alpujarras to the Axarquía, where Andrés el-Chorairán, from Sedella, whipped up the emotions of his people and a Christian inn was attacked. This provoked brutal reprisals by the authorities.

The inhabitants of the Axarquía could take no more and rallied to the banner raised by Francisco

15

Roxas at Canillas de Aceituno. Not for nothing was this region said to have been populated by "slight, strong men of such great spirit that in the old days the Moorish kings regarded them as the most valiant, daring and effective in the Kingdom of Granada".

To crush the rebellion, Felipe II's forces were reinforced with troops sent from Italy. Thousands of men disembarked on the beaches of Torrox and advanced on Frigiliana where the rebels and their families had taken refuge in the castle and on the adjacent mountain, El Fuerte.

A decisive battle was fought on June 11, 1569. The Moriscos put up a desperate resistance, rolling rocks down on their adversaries, but had no hope. At least 2,000 Moriscos died, against 400 losses on the Christian side.

Thousands of Moriscos were ejected from their land and decamped to north Africa. They were replaced by Christian settlers from other regions. The Inquisition scrutinised the population for signs of heresy, forcing those Muslims and Jews who had not fled to convert to Catholicism, or at least to feign conversion. Business enterprise diminished, irrigation systems were abandoned, agriculture went into decline and centuries passed before Andalusia recovered.

Battling Napoleon

Between the ejection of the Moors and the Napoleonic Wars Spain suffered under a series of sadly inept monarchs — the enlightened Carlos III stood out like a beacon among them. Meanwhile, Málaga and Granada provinces had their quota of natural disasters, crop failures, epidemics and earthquakes. Along the coast there was the constant threat from Barbary pirates. Most villages had little contact with the outside world, except when their young men were pressed into service in some distant war or the tax collector made his impositions — Cervantes was one such visitor.

The 19th-century was one of the most turbulent in local history. When Napoleon's forces occupied the country, guerrilla units waged war against them. In the region east of Málaga Tío Caridad, mayor of Otívar, led one guerrilla band and the priest of Riogordo led another. Ambushes and violent reprisals were common.

While the guerrillas hounded the French then retreated to refuges in the mountains, British and Portuguese forces under the Duke of Wellington marched across the peninsula, scoring a series of victories against Napoleon's armies. The British navy bombarded fortresses held by the French at Torrox, Nerja and Almuñécar.

Conditions did not improve after the War of Independence when the tyrannical Fernando VII was crowned king. Many guerrillas became outlaws and terrorised the country. They were following an old tradition in Andalusia. Rebels and outlaws have always run off to the sierras and in Moorish times bandits known as monfíes harassed country folk.

One highwayman haunting the Axarquía was the notorious El Tempranillo, who allegedly claimed that "the king may rule in Spain but in the sierra I do". (See entry on Alfarnate.) Later came three of the region's most feared bandits: El Bizco of El Borge, El Melgares of Algarrobo and Frasco Antonio of Vélez-Málaga. Unsurprisingly, they met violent deaths.

A disastrous earthquake on Christmas Day, 1884, desolated parts of Málaga and Granada provinces, causing hundreds of deaths. A Málaga newspaper repor-

Sketch of bandolero

ted: "The earthquake has caused havoc in all the picturesque villages in the area. In the mountains huge rocks, shaken from their position, have rolled in furious avalanche down the slopes, producing as much damage as the earth tremors."

Twenty-six tremors hit Torrox in two hours and terror-stricken Nerja inhabitants took to the beaches as houses and a church collapsed. But Granada was much worse hit. At Albuñuelas in the Lecrín valley more than 100 people died and survivors took refuge in caves from a fierce storm.

As if this disaster was not enough, an economic crisis was provoked by the *phylloxera* plague which wiped out southern Spain's wine industry in the late 19th-century. Poverty was a way of life in this region where illiteracy was the norm and feudal conditions prevailed.

Sugar cane was the most important coastal industry, dominated by the Marqués de Larios and family. These days the Larios company's real estate branch, known as Salsa, plants apartment blocks rather than cane and its vast tracts of land have soared in value thanks to the tourist boom.

FLIGHT FROM MÁLAGA

When Laurie Lee trekked along the coast in 1935, he noted the "salt-fish villages, thin-ribbed, sea-hating, cursing their place in the sun". The Civil War, 1936-39, brought more suffering. When Málaga was taken by the Nationalists in 1937, thousands of families fled along the coast road towards Motril and Almería. Warships and aircraft bombarded them in their desperate flight.

The scene was recorded by Norman Bethune, an heroic Canadian doctor who organised a mobile blood transfusion service for the Republican army. He observed "a silent, haggard, tortured flood of men and animals" tottering along what is today the N340. "Dying burros had been pushed on to the beaches below, where people lay stretched in exhaustion, their swollen tongues hanging from puckered mouths."

Then followed the long dictatorship of General Franco, aptly dubbed "a sphinx without a secret". Although Franco supposedly brought peace, thousands of Spaniards were executed in the early years of his regime. And from 1943 to 1952 the Axarquía and parts of Granada province were embroiled in another brutal conflict.

GUERRILLA WAR

On moonless nights in 1943 and 1944 small craft edged stealthily into secluded coves along Spain's Málaga and Granada coastline and armed men leaped ashore. Secretly trained in North Africa, they were the spearhead of a guerrilla movement aimed at undermining Franco's ruthless dictatorship, in the belief that — once Hitler and Mussolini were crushed — the Allies would sweep south across the Pyrenees.

They disembarked in the bays of La Caleta, Cantarriján and Cerro Gordo between Nerja and Almuñécar and moved into the sierras via the Río de la Miel. That valley, traditionally a refuge for smugglers, became a breeding ground of resistance, to the point where it was called "Little Russia".

Although they had seriously considered invading Spain, the Allies never did oust Franco — a second betrayal, following their refusal to act during the Civil War. But the guerrillas continued their campaign until the early 1950s. It was a bitter conflict, which went largely unreported inside and outside Spain.

A charismatic leader, know as El Roberto, created a mini-army of up to 150 guerrillas. Although the leaders were convinced Communists, the rest were a mixture of idealistic Republicans, anarchists, outlaws and naïve village youths attracted by the adventure. Opposing them were the Civil Guard, soldiers and police.

Guerrillas-Venta Panaderos

Caught in the middle were the villagers of the Axarquía and Granada, many of whom had sons, brothers and husbands in the mountains. Repression by Franco's forces was merciless while the guerrillas killed anybody suspected of betrayal. In desperation, many people emigrated to Barcelona and abroad.

High in the sierras, the Venta Panaderos entered into local legend. Today the inn is in ruins, but then its situation below the Frigiliana Pass made it a meeting point for all those who travelled between Málaga and Granada provinces. Muleteers would gulp down a drink there before tackling the stiff climb up to the pass.

One moment the Civil Guard would enter and the next the guerrillas. On at least one occasion the guards entered the inn to find food being prepared for a large number of men, meals ordered by the guerrillas. The guards shrugged and proceeded to scoff the food themselves.

Few of the guerrillas survived, many being killed "while trying to escape". The final blow came when El Roberto was arrested and, during months of interrogation, betrayed his remaining comrades in the sierras. He and his closest aides were executed.

Even now he is a subject of controversy. For some he remains an icon of the anti-Franco struggle, for others a contemptible traitor. And others insist he never was executed, but did a deal with his interrogators and was allowed to flee to South America. What is certain is that the guerrilla war scarred the Axarquía for generations.

Tourism takes off

From the 1960s a new era opened with the arrival of new invaders. They weren't interested in politics. Sunshine and cheap living were the attractions. The Costa del Sol began to take off. Initially, little changed in the eastern section but in the new millennium the coast from Málaga to Motril and beyond has experienced an unprecedented boom. Thousands of villas and apartments have been constructed, mostly to accommodate north European sun-seekers.

Agriculture, which until recently employed 20 per cent of the work force, is fast losing ground to tourism. Construction has become a major industry, employing more than 25 per cent of the workers, and raising fears that over-building may destroy some of the region's charm.

While initially tourism development concentrated on the coast, a new phenomenon made itself felt during the 1990s: rural tourism. Hundreds of old farmhouses and village dwellings have been renovated to provide accommodation for city-dwellers eager to escape modern stress and for those who prefer outdoor rural activities to lounging on a beach.

Thousands of north Europeans have either bought second homes or arrived to live permanently under the sun. Hundreds more have come to provide the services they demand, from fitting solar panels to mending the

Ploughing

Hikers-Axarquía

plumbing. Most newcomers want a view of the sea or, failing that, of a lake. Thus the Viñuela reservoir, north of Vélez-Málaga, has acted like a magnet in drawing British settlers inland.

Apart from Rincón de la Victoria (a dormitory town for Málaga), there are only two major centres of any size: Vélez-Málaga, market town and "capital" of the Axarquía, and Motril, port and administrative focus of the Costa Tropical.

Of the resorts, high-rise Torre del Mar attracts both Spanish and foreign (mainly German) tourists by the thousands and Torrox-Costa has a strong German presence. The British have descended en masse on Nerja. Inland, Scandinavians and British have settled in large numbers around Cómpeta.

The Spanish are still holding their own in Almuñécar, the chief tourist resort of the Costa Tropical, and Salobreña to the east. In inland Granada, the Lecrín valley has attracted a growing community of British.

As concrete threatens to blight a place of beauty, some newcomers — mindful or not that they are part of the problem — raise anguished voices. But it's well to remember how it was in the good old days.

Back in the 1960s, when the cement-mixers were already working overtime between Málaga and Gibraltar and package tourists were flocking to exotic new destinations like Torremolinos and Marbella, the Axarquía still slumbered. Land was selling at two pesetas a square metre, wine was 10 pesetas a litre, a three-course meal could be had for 60 pesetas. Artists, hippies, dropouts drifted in, crying: "This is paradise."

But not for the locals. Fishermen and farmers survived on a diet of poverty and resignation. Roads were pitted with potholes. The villages had no qualified dentists nor ambulances. The fine regional hospital near Torre del Mar was not even a dream. Accident victims were bundled into a taxi for a painful, jolting ride into Málaga (not until foreign residents raised the funds did Nerja acquire its first ambulance).

In this context, present-day attitudes of axarquicos and granadinos eager for more development are easier to understand. One can only hope they will heed the advice of King Juan Carlos. Visiting this area in June, 1998, he was impressed by the charms of the villages and commented to one mayor: "You have a very pretty pueblo. Do everything to conserve it."

LEGACY OF THE MOORS

The long arm of Al-Andalus reaches down the centuries to touch us. It influences the music we hear, the food we eat, the language we speak. The Moors (a term covering both Arabs and Berbers) brought to Europe the aubergine and the Arabian steed but also a new view of Aristotle, of astronomy and of medicine.

Moorish influence is particularly strong in the Axarquía and Granada province for they dominated southern Spain for nearly 800 years. Locals are only half joking when they say: "We're all Moors here."

When one opens his mouth, his debt is obvious. Such words as *alcachofa, alcázar, alforja, alguacil, arroz, aduana, alcalde, naranja, azúcar* and *limón* all came from the invaders. And so too did those "English" words like cotton (from *algodón*), alcohol, elixir, nadir, zenith, almanac, zero, jasmine, saffron, coffee.

All through the region you will come across traces of Moorish culture: churches with towers originally built as minarets (Archez has a fine example), village names like Alcaucín, Benamocarra and Benaudalla, typical archways, ingenious *acequias* (water channels).

Américo Castro, the eminent historian, pointed out that Spain owes its character as a nation to three peoples, Muslims, Jews and Christians. The ousting of the first two inflicted wounds from which Spain took centuries to recover, but it could not root out a lasting influence.

While the Roman aqueducts improved water supplies to settlements, it was the Moors who developed an intricate system of irrigation which revolutionised agricultural production. Experts in harnessing water for domestic and agricultural use, they constructed *aljibes* (rain-collecting tanks), *albercas* (cisterns), *acequias* (irrigation channels) and *norias* (water wheels). Those words are still in use as are many of the Moorish waterways.

Previously unproductive mountainous areas could be populated. Fruit and vegetables previously unknown were introduced, such as bananas, almonds, apricots, peaches, aubergines and cucumbers, along with sorghum and hemp. Silkworms feasted on large plantations of mulberry trees. Sugar refineries were established along the southern coast.

Water power was the main source of electricity for many villages until recently and one or two Moorish water-powered mills are still in working order. Until irrigation piping was installed, the sound of running water was one of the commonest in the countryside.

An intense belief in human contact, the love of flowery language, a flair for flamboyance, the lack of inhibition about enjoying the moment, a cavalier attitude towards time, all can probably be traced to the Moorish heritage.

When you travel the Axarquía, the Costa Tropical, the Lecrín valley and the Alpujarras, you can also see considerable physical evidence of the Moorish era, from crumbling castle walls to horseshoe arches and colourful ceramics. Countless churches were built on the foundations of mosques, some retaining the minarets.

Muslim craftsmen who worked under Christian rule produced the influential style known as Mudejar (from *mudayyan*, the subjected one). In many churches in Málaga and Granada this style, which features elaborate brickwork and glazed tiles, has been overlaid with baroque decorations. Examples are to be found at Cútar, Comares, Vélez-Málaga, Salobreña and many more villages. The intricate coffered ceiling, to be found in numerous buildings, was a speciality of Mudejar builders.

Village sunset

The supreme example of Moorish architecture was built in Granada during the Nasrid Dynasty. Resembling a dream from *A Thousand and One Nights*, the Alhambra (the red fort) dazzles the eye with its alabaster pilasters, ethereal arches and icing-sugar cupolas while the ear is lulled by the melody of running water. Guitar maestro Andrés Segovia, who had a home on the Costa Tropical, described Granada as a "place of dreams, where Our Lord put the seed of music in my soul".

A humbler example of Moorish architecture is the traditional Alpujarras dwelling. This has a flat roof of beams overlaid with slate slabs and a layer of rubble, the same style as the Berber houses of Morocco. Old village houses of Málaga and Granada are constructed of compacted mud and stone with typically Moorish roof tiles, one end broader than the other.

Walk through one of the weekly markets and you will likely see on sale ceramics with designs of clear Moorish influence, such as Fajalauza pottery — characterised by birds and pomegranates in blue and green glazes — turned out by the *alfareros* (another Arab word) of Granada.

If your children mutter about the intricacies of algebra (al-jabr, the binding together of parts), remind them how lucky they are that the Arabs introduced their own numerals in place of the unwieldy Roman system.

Arabs were using such navigational aids as the compass long before Europeans. Indeed, Columbus evolved his theories about a new route to the East after consulting early Arab charts such as the world map produced by the geographer al-Idrisi in 1154.

Even the order in which we eat a meal may be traced to the Moors. A number of culinary refinements were devised by Ziryab, an extraordinary ninth-century musician at the caliph's court in Córdoba. He initiated a new fashion, ordaining that courses were no longer served haphazard but in strict order, sweets, fruit and nuts coming last.

Many ultra-sweet desserts beloved by Spaniards and such dishes as gazpacho and *ajo blanco* are a legacy too, while such Arab-style dishes as lamb cooked with honey are being revived.

The next time you hear a guitar take a moment to wonder how it would sound with only four strings. Ziryab introduced the fifth string to the Arab lute, contributing to its development into the six-string guitar.

Oriental influences helped shape flamenco music. James Woodall in his book In Search of the Firedance theorises that the word flamenco may come from felagmengu, meaning "fugitive peasant", or fela men eikum, an Andalusian worker of the Moorish era.

The passion and pain of *cante jondo* recall Arab song and the saeta, that "arrow" of adulation launched at the Virgin in Semana Santa, is almost an echo of the cries of praise that the faithful make to Allah. When the Arabs recited such poetry, listeners would cry out "wa-Allah!" at the end of each stanza, just as today flamenco fans call out "Olé!".

Once a word in the ear of the sultan or vizier was the only way to ensure action. So today, rather than email or phone a person of influence, Andalusians believe/know personal connections are all.

And then there is the matter of time. "We do not see virtue in doing things fast," says José, a gypsy poet from Granada. "Everything should be enjoyed slowly. Like a pass in a bullfight."

NATURE PARKS

Ramblers, bird-watchers, nature-lovers are in luck. Three areas covered by this guide enjoy special protection as they have been declared nature parks. No concrete and precious few humans.

On the Axarquía's western flank, north of the city of Málaga, are the Montes de Málaga and on the coast, where Málaga and Granada provinces meet, is the Paraje Natural Acantilados Maro-Cerro Gordo (see special sections). The largest and most important park is that formed by the Tejeda and Almijara mountain ranges.

Hiking up waterfall

SHIELDING THE COAST

Covering 40,000 hectares with peaks soaring more than 2,000 metres above sea level, the Parque Natural de las Sierras Tejeda y Almijara forms a formidable barrier that shields the Málaga and Granada coasts from wintry blasts. Ancient earth movements and millennia of erosion have carved razor-sharp ridges and deep gullies, sinkholes and caves (that at Nerja is a spectacular example, but many more await discovery).

Parts of these mountains are composed of gneiss, schist and quartz dating back 500 million years. More predominant are the dolomitic marbles which originated in marine depths during the Triassic period, a mere 300 million years back. The water runs off quickly, gathering in aquifers far below the surface. Where it emerges, settlements have been established since early times.

The highest peak is the Maroma (see separate section) but others are equally as striking. Atop El Lucero, also known as El Raspón de los Moriscos (which could be translated as the Moorish skyscraper), stand the remains of a Civil Guard lookout post. Above Nerja, El Cielo rules in monolithic splendour.

For long these mountains were the refuge of rebels and runaways. Moorish outlaws used to roam them. Guerrillas emerged from them to battle Napoleon's troops. For a time in the 19th-century the bandoleros ruled the sierras. After the Spanish Civil War, guerrillas hid out here as they tried to topple the Franco dictatorship.

Once the sierras hummed with activity. Mule trains, smugglers, blackmarketeers and travelling salesmen plodded the stony paths, steep and sinuous, which cross the mountains, linking small villages in Málaga and Granada provinces.

Goatherds, charcoal-burners, wood-cutters, lime kiln workers, miners, quarrymen and collectors of esparto grass and pine resin made use of the resources. Fires have destroyed many trees, the most disastrous occurring in 1975 — it wiped out thousands of pines prompting the closure of a large resin treatment plant near Fornes (Granada).

Today you can hike, mountain-bike or horse-ride all day and glimpse not one other human. You will find abandoned farmhouses and inns, places with names like Cortijo del Imán, Cueva del Daire and Venta Panaderos. Only a few kilometres inland from the Costa del Sol your only companions may be wild goats, a cruising eagle and soaring vultures.

Pines, boxwood, oaks, juniper, wild olives draw sustenance from the thin soils of the limestone ranges. Clover, thyme, rosemary, sage, wild asparagus, lavender, rockroses clothe the slopes, particularly in spring.

The name "Tejeda" is believed to derive from a small type of yew tree

Horse trekking

which once grew in abundance. "Almijara" is believed to originate in the Arabic "almijar", meaning "draining board", possibly alluding to the fast run-off.

Hikers will more than likely catch glimpses of the *cabra montés*, especially in the early morning or evening near water. Although poachers still take a toll, stricter controls have helped boost the goat population to an estimated 1,500 on the Málaga side of the sierras alone, ten times the total 25 years ago. A male goat can live up to 20 years and, fully grown, weighs around 75 kilos with horns up to a metre long.

Recently the common squirrel has proliferated through the sierras and the wild boar has made a comeback. Lizards and grass snakes are common, the viper there but rarely seen. Wildcats, foxes and rabbits are other residents and by night you may see badgers sneaking across the back roads. The last wolf disappeared around 1900.

OUTDOOR ACTIVITIES

The sea and mountains east of Málaga are ideal for those seeking an active holiday. Along the coast you can enjoy every sport from sailing, scuba-diving and snorkelling to windsurfing and water-skiing. Five golf courses are within easy reach, as are the ski slopes of the Sierra Nevada.

Canyoning addicts head for the Río Verde valley, behind Almuñécar, a splendour of sheer cliffs and thundering water. Paragliders and hang-gliders find no shortage of suitable launch pads from the mountains behind Maro, Almuñécar and other points along the coast. The rocky inlets between Almuñécar and Nerja are ideal for snorkellers and scuba-divers.

Facilities are available for exploring the back country on horseback or mountain bike. And, whether you are fit enough to challenge the high sierras or prefer to wander between sleepy, whitewashed villages, the Axarquía and the Costa Tropical hinterland offer ideal hiking country.

Fairly gentle walks can be made through the foothills just in from the coast, a landscape of vineyards and olive groves and terraced fields where tropical fruits flourish. Several fairly easy walks of one to three hours can be made in the Montes de Málaga, starting from the Lagar de Torrijos and the Aula de la Naturaleza Las Contadoras.

The more adventurous will find outlets for their energy in the Sierras Almijara and Tejeda and, to the east in Granada province, the Sierra del Chaparral. Abrupt limestone ridges, deep ravines and hidden caves characterise this region, perfect for mountain goats, runaways — and hikers.

The paths through the mountains were once major highways, traversed day and night by man and mule. Now many are abandoned and overgrown, some impossible to find, but efforts are being made to improve and signpost them.

Be warned, however, that the information boards marking the start of many walks are not always reliable. You may find the word "Mentira!" on some boards, scrawled there by angry hikers who have discovered the estimated walking times are way too optimistic.

Spring and autumn are ideal times for walking this region, but — as it enjoys the mildest climate in Europe — winter too offers magnificent days. February can be especially scenic, when almond blossom cloaks hillsides in what at first sight appears to be a mantle of snow.

Good maps (see Practicalities), a compass and sturdy footwear are essential for sierra walking. Never under-estimate the mountains. Even the simplest walk can prove hazardous if the weather changes. It can be sunny and clear on the coast when a storm is raking the mountain-tops. Be sure to check the weather forecast before starting out and make an early start.

MÁLAGA'S HOLY MOUNTAIN

Look inland from the beaches of the Axarquía and you see rising impressively in the distance what at first seems like a mirage — the massive bulk of the

Maroma. At 2,068 metres, this is the highest peak in Málaga province and it exerts a strong pull on popular imagination.

It's probably the closest thing to a holy mountain in these parts and quite a few *malagueños* dream of hiking to the summit at least once in their lifetimes. Some make a point of sleeping there at the summer solstice so as to see the dawn.

Their feelings are reflected in a plaque at the summit which records: "Here and now ends an ascent/Here and how begins another./This mountain is the centre of the world./This mountain unites land and sky./This mountain like any mountain is a a sacred place./That's why you are here…"

Down from Maroma

In winter the Maroma is blanketed in snow. At any time of year it may be wreathed in cloud. In summer, while sun-worshippers crowd the torrid coast, sudden storms can whip across its rocky, treeless slopes.

In the days before refrigeration the *neveros* (literally, "snowmen") would trek to the top of Maroma to seek snow and ice. This they would pack hard in straw and load it in esparto baskets on the backs of mules. Transported to the coast, the ice was used to cool drinks or make ice-cream.

High up the mountain you can still see the *casa de la nieve* (house of snow), or rather its ruins, where snow was stored. Indeed, the name of this mountain stems — or so it is said — from the collection of ice from sinkholes,

Maroma summit

deep crevices 40 to 50 metres deep. The only way to reach the ice was by shinning down ropes, or *maromas*.

The most popular route to the summit follows the path once used to bring down ice from the snow pits far above. It starts from Canillas de Aceituno, climbs some 1,400 metres and takes around 10 hours of serious hiking there and back.

Another route begins from the Alcázar recreation area near the village of Alcaucín. This hike takes at least seven hours, starting at 850 metres above sea-level.

Perhaps the most agreeable and scenic way up starts in Granada province from a camping area known as El Robledal, off the Ventas de Zafarraya road to Alhama de Granada. The first section passes through forests of pines, yews and maples.

From Maroma's summit, a bleak plateau of rock, you enjoy tremendous views in all directions. The Asociación Excursionista de la Axarquía has placed a box where visitors leave names and comments while others have inscribed their names on the pillar, a trig point. This point is actually in Granada province, but that doesn't stop malagueños claiming the mountain as their own.

FOOD, GLORIOUS FOOD

Richard Ford had some useful culinary advice for the traveller in his book *Gatherings from Spain*. "A prudent man will always victual himself in Spain with vivers for three days at least," he suggested. And he should employ a versatile cook who "must set forth from every tolerable-sized town with an ample supply of tea, sugar, coffee, brandy, good oil, wine, salt, to say nothing of solids."

But that was nearly 200 years ago. Life is simpler these days and the food supply abundant, particularly in the Axarquía and the Costa Tropical. Fresh local produce is a feature of the local cuisine. Olive oil, garlic and peppers are traditional ingredients, but the region also produces a variety of delicious tropical fruits — avocados, mangos, custard apples — which have been incorporated into the diet.

Fresh fish is featured at beach restaurants all along the coast of Málaga and Granada. Sardines barbecued on sticks stuck in the sand and platefuls of fried fish, including squid, hake, red mullet and anchovies, are popular. Gourmets along the Costa Tropical can't have enough *quisquillas* of Motril, a particular type of shrimp.

Village menus often offer *choto con papas a lo pobre* (kid with fried potatoes). Roast, fried or stewed, baby goat is prized as a true feast — in the past only served on special occasions — and hearty stews, including chunks of pork or chicken, are often on the menu. Thus, Alfarnatejo prides itself on its *cocido de garbanzos* (chickpea stew), Iznate on its pots of runner beans and chickpeas, Canillas de Albaida and Cómpeta on their fennel stews.

Sedella boasts of its *choto al vino* (kid cooked in wine) and Periana of its dishes made with peaches. Gazpacho is a popular summer soup and also *ajoblanco* (cold almond soup), to which the village of Almáchar devotes a special fiesta.

Moorish-style dishes such as roast lamb coated in honey (the bees feed on rosemary and thyme in the sierras) are making a comeback in more innovative restaurants.

Usually fresh fruit is the best bet for dessert. Ultra-sweet pastries *(pestiños, roscos and mantecados)* are popular, particularly at Christmas.

Motril's special dessert, known as Torta Real, originated with the Moors. It achieved national fame and royal approval during the reign of Alfonso XIII. Ingredients include almonds, egg whites and sugar, but the exact recipe remains a secret, zealously guarded by one family for some 200 years.

Local produce features in quite a few fiestas. Canillas de Aceituno has a Black Pudding Day and Colmenar celebrates wine and pork products. Torrox goes overboard at the annual *migas* festivities.

In the past a conch shell would be blown to inform olive-pickers that lunch was served and they would troop to the *cortijos* to dig into portions of *migas*, a belly-filling dish made with flour or bread crumbs, guaranteed to satisfy a manual worker's appetite though it may not excite more sophisticated palates.

(See Where to eat, under Practicalities, for recommended restaurants.)

PLOUGHMAN'S BRUNCH

Traditionally, *migas* (for two persons) requires a quarter glass of olive oil, five garlic cloves, a glass of water, a glass of flour and salt. But mathematical precision in measuring out ingredients is not necessary, say the locals. After browning the garlic in the oil in a paella pan, you add water and salt and, when the mixture starts boiling, toss in the flour. Stir until all is cooked and the flour breaks up into crumbs.

In the Torrox area, it is usually served with a salad, consisting of oranges, tomatoes, onions, cod, olives, olive oil, salt and vinegar. But it is also eaten with fried fish.

Bottled sunshine

Málaga has probably the longest history of wine-making in Spain and in the hills of the Axarquía you can find farmers producing the local vintage with methods that have barely changed in centuries. While vineyards have been ripped up to plant more profitable crops, such as tropical fruits and second homes, the vines still clothe many a precipitous slope.

Málaga can boast that it was the first region to set standards by creating a *"denominación de origen"*. That was in 1933, but vines are believed to have been cultivated here as far back as Phoenician times.

It was the thirsty Romans who created many of the first vineyards, importing and planting numerous new varieties of grape. Columella, a Roman poet and agriculturalist, wrote about the area's vines in the first century AD and Pliny and Virgil sang Málaga wine's praises.

The Moors cultivated vines to produce raisins, but they also produced "xarab al malaqui" (Málaga syrup). They were prohibited from drinking alcohol so this sweet wine was made "for medicinal purposes". That they appreciated its qualities is evidenced in lines written by al-Mutamid, the 11th-century ruler of Seville: "As I was passing by a vine/Its tendrils tugged my sleeve./'Do you intend,' said I,/'My body so to grieve?'/'Why do you pass?' replied the vine,/'And never greeting make?/It took this blood of mine/Your thirsting bones to slake.'"

Back in 1502 the Catholic Monarchs took the first known measure to protect a regional wine from imported products. A century later Málaga wine-producers formed a guild, the fore-runner of today's consejos reguladores (control boards).

The fame of Málaga wine spread across the seas. The Sultan of Samarkand is said to have sent a carrack to the city to pick up a cargo of wine, and Catherine the Great of Russia was also a fan. Thousands of litres of wine and tons of raisins were exported annually, much of it to Latin America but also to Britain. The wine export business brought many British to the city of Málaga, as it also did to Jerez and Oporto.

Noting that the local economy depended on the vineyards, the Reverend Joseph Townsend commented in 1787 on the hard labour involved: "In no other country on earth are the workers so uncomplaining about heat, hunger and thirst, or capable of greater sacrifices than those here, yet who are often painted as lazy people…"

Preparing raisins

At that time there were 14,000 wine presses. But in the late 19th- century the flourishing trade was dealt a death blow by a little bug known as the phylloxera. It wiped out entire vineyards. The Montes de Málaga, north of the provincial capital, never recovered and the whole area has been planted with trees.

On top of that came a change in tastes. Dry wines are "in", sweet wines are "out". No matter how delicious the Málaga wines are they are difficult to market to a fashion-obsessed world.

Whereas once there were more than 100,000 hectares of vineyards in the province, today there are only 6,000 hectares. Of those about 1,000 hectares produce eating grapes and the remaining area is split between production for wine and raisins. Most of the wine comes from the Mollina area, near Antequera, and most of the raisins come from the Axarquía.

Many small farmers in the Axarquía make wine only for family needs, treading the grapes in the traditional, laborious way. They sell off any surplus, so your best guarantee of obtaining genuine local wine is to buy it from villagers who advertise with signs outside their houses.

Although the Pedro Ximénez grape is commonly used in Málaga province to produce sweet wines, the typical wine of the Axarquía is a sweet, full-bodied Moscatel, yellow to amber in colour, with 16 or 17 per cent alcohol. It is perfect as a dessert wine, although drier varieties are made too.

To boost sugar and thus alcohol content, the Moscatel grapes are sunned before being crushed. Outside many farmhouses in the Axarquía you will see *paseros*, beds where every autumn the freshly-picked grapes are laid out on slopes facing the sun. At night they are covered to protect them from the dew.

Cómpeta is most famed for its traditional Málaga wine and celebrates the fact with a wine festival in August. Every other village, however, is convinced that its wine is the best and insists that, unlike its rivals, theirs "has no chemicals added".

Most of the vines in the Axarquía are devoted to the production of sun-dried raisins. For long, the raisins were at a disadvantage on international markets, particularly when they had to compete with seedless raisins from Israel. But marketing has been stepped up to improve exports.

In fact, the Axarquía grapes, seeds or not, are some of the most luscious and mouth-watering you could hope to taste. For an idea of the work involved in producing them visit the Museo de la Pasa in Almáchar.

Several bodegas in the Axarquía and in the Contraviesa in Granada province are working on a true break-through: the production of palatable red and white table wines, hitherto unknown in this zone. Among the pioneers are a Dutch couple. Their winery near Sayalonga makes a red from the Romé grape, almost certainly first introduced by the Romans. Innovators are also experimenting in Almáchar, Moclinejo and other villages.

See also "Contraviesa's new image".

Fiestas

Overwhelming fiestas, minor fiestas, oddball fiestas, newly invented fiestas, ancient fiestas…the Axarquía and the Costa Tropical have them all. Some will flee from the crowds and noise associated with many of these events, but there are festivities to interest everyone.

Colourful processions parade through towns and cities during the Cabalgata de Reyes on January 5. The Three Kings, sometimes mounted on camels, throw caramels and other gifts to the children.

Carnival (Carnaval in Spanish) in February is the signal for an outburst of revelry in which normally sedate citizens deck themselves in outrageous costumes and parade through the streets chanting songs, which range from the satirical to the scurrilous, about local and national personalities. The final day they take part in the so-called Burial of the Sardine, an excuse for more feasting and dancing.

Semana Santa, a major holiday in Spain, is marked in Andalusia with sumptuous processions in every community. To thundering drums religious images are paraded through the streets, accompanied by hooded penitents. The mixture of solemn Christian devotion and pagan festivity cannot fail to impress a visitor — or at least send a chill up and down the spine.

Romeria

Nerja-Virgen del Carmen

Processions take place from Palm Sunday onwards, climaxing on Good Friday, but some communities hold Easter Sunday processions too. Vélez-Málaga probably has the most sumptuous examples of solemn pomp and semi-pagan ecstasy in the Axarquía. Riogordo goes one better than other villages by staging *El Paso*, a passion play, with a cast of more than 500.

The little village of Cajiz (exit the A7 autoroute at km265 and go 1.7km north on the MA3203, direction Iznate and Benamocarra) also stages a passion play on Good Friday and Easter Saturday, in which 200 inhabitants take part.

May 3, the Día de la Cruz, is celebrated with colourful spring festivities in many towns and villages. Neighbours decorate corners of their barrios (quarters), erecting crosses adorned with flowers and offer refreshment to passers-by.

Corpus Christi, in May or June, is celebrated with solemn church services and religious processions, householders draping colourful shawls or bedspreads over their balconies.

The shortest night of the year, June 23, is the excuse for an all-night party at beaches all along the coast from Rincón to Torre del Mar, Torrox-Costa, Nerja, Almuñecar, Salobreña and beyond. The sparks fly high from scores of bonfires and sardines grilled on spits are consumed by the thousand as visitors and natives celebrate the summer solstice. At the magic hour of midnight everybody takes to the water, a cleansing operation to ensure good fortune in the year ahead. Women who wash their faces with salt water at this moment will become prettier and the unmarried who plunge into the sea will surely find novios and marry before the year's end.

The Virgen del Carmen has her day on July 16 when fishermen pay homage to their patron in numerous towns, including Rincón de la Victoria, Torre del Mar, Nerja and Salobreña. Images of the Virgin are hoisted aboard fishing boats for marine processions, usually accompanied by an explosion of fireworks.

In addition to national and regional holidays, every community celebrates its patron saint's day. The festivities can go on for up to a week, with fun fair, pop concerts, folk dances, flamenco and a certain amount of drinking. Usually there is a *romería*, a pilgrimage to a shrine in which religious images are paraded through the village, town and the countryside.

But there are many other festivities, some celebrating a particular local product, others commemorating historic events and some newly created to attract tourists.

Struggles between Moors and Christians are remembered in ceremonies from Alfarnate in the high Axarquía to Béznar in the Lecrín valley. Almuñécar commemorates an event in 1569 when Felipe II's troops repelled an attempt by the Morisco leader Aben Humeya to take the castle. The Virgen de la Antigua is embarked in a fishing craft and paraded along the waterfront amid a spectacular fireworks display.

Moorish outlaws *(monfíes)* get their turn at little Cútar, which holds a Fiesta del Monfí every October. In the spring of 2007 Frigiliana introduced an international belly-dancing festival and in August it celebrates Tres Culturas, during which restaurants serve examples of the Muslim, Christian and Jewish cuisines.

One of the Axarquía's most popular fiestas is Cómpeta's Noche del Vino, a celebration of the local Moscatel wine. But many other localities have initiated festivals honouring such specialities as gazpacho (Alfarnatejo),

Romería dancers

garlic and almond soup (Almáchar), raisins (El Borge), blood sausage (Canillas de Aceituno), pork (Colmenar), olive oil (Periana), *nísperos* or medlar (Sayalonga), stew (Totalán).

Possibly the Axarquía's biggest crowd-puller is staged just before Christmas at Torrox. Held every year since 1981, the Fiesta de las Migas attracts vast crowds — 40,000 by some estimates.

They tuck into free platefuls of migas (see section on Traditional Dishes for the ingredients) washed down by vast quantities of local wine.

Singing shepherds are a feature of the Christmas scene. Garbed in sheep and goatskins and accompanied by young girls in traditional dress, the groups play castanets, tambourines, bells and *zambombas* (a drum played by rubbing a stick embedded in a taut skin).

The *pastorales*, an ancient custom dating back centuries, have staged a revival in recent years. The singers parade through village streets, play at some church services and also take part in the processions at Reyes (Festival of the Three Kings). Often new carols *(villancicos)* are specially composed for the groups to sing, some strictly religious, others making comic references to local people and customs.

Apart from the traditonal-style fiestas, listed under each community's entry, a number of towns stage special festivals. Among them are: Almuñécar — July, International Jazz Festival; Nerja — end of June, International Music and Dance Festival; Vélez-Málaga — end of November, Jazz, Rhythm and Blues Festival.

OLIVE-PICKERS' LULLABY

Outrageous headgear, driving rhythms and twirling flags are features of the unusual music known as *verdiales*. The pandas, as the groups are known, play at many fiestas in the Montes de Málaga and the Axarquía.

Don't expect anything like flamenco, although there is a similarity to the fandango. Smartly attired in black pants and white shirts with red cummerbunds, the groups play guitars, fiddles, castanets, cymbals and tambourines with rare abandon. Listening to the music may feel like being clubbed, repeatedly, with a sharp instrument but the primitive style certainly has a hypnotic effect.

According to one theory, the *verdiales* sprang from the songs of the olive-pickers in Moorish times (the verdial is a variety of olive), though some say they date back to the time of Pompey — a mosaic in that doomed city shows musicians wearing similar hats. Think of Carmen Miranda colliding with a Christmas tree and you can envisage the headgear, composed of plastic flowers, mirrors, beads and long ribbons.

Led by an *"alcalde"* (mayor), the pandas compete with one another in wild bursts of music while up to three members, men and women, perform whirling dances. The *"abanderado"* twirls a lar-ge flag in complicated patterns. The singers tell of rural romance and other incidents.

Verdiales band-Torrox

There are three styles of verdiales: that of Almogía (with the fastest beat), of Comares (the only one employing the lute) and of the Montes (with a slightly slower rhythm). You can hear/witness all three at the biggest verdiales festival held every December 28 at the Venta de San Cayetano, Puerto de la Torre, just outside Málaga. Thousands of fans turn up for a skull-blasting bacchanal involving dozens of pandas competing for prizes and vast quantities of pork sausages and wine.

A similar, Moorish-influenced music endures in the Alpujarras, el trovo. See under Murtas in the section on the Contraviesa.

Verdiales dancers

EXPLORING
THE AXARQUÍA

Vélez-Málaga

MONTES DE MÁLAGA

FRINGING the western edge of the Axarquía (north-east of the city of Málaga) lie thickly forested hills known as the Montes de Málaga, 4,995 hectares of which are protected as a nature park.

Vineyards clothed many of these ridges rising above the Guadalmedina valley, producing sweet, potent Málaga wine which enjoyed international fame. But in the late 19th-century disaster struck. The *phylloxera*, a small bug, attacked the vines and delivered a deadly blow to the local wine industry from which it has never fully recovered. Vines formerly covered 100,000 hectares in the province: now there are about 6,000 hectares, of which only 20 per cent are devoted to wine production and the rest to raisins.

Centuries ago the whole area was forested. But when the Catholic Monarchs doled out estates, the trees were felled to allow the cultivation of oats, olives, almonds and vines. As a result, there was nothing to stop rainwater quickly running off into the Guadalmedina and Málaga suffered disastrous floods.

However, last century, after the vineyards were abandoned, thousands of pines were planted to serve as a protective barrier. Now native species, such as holm and cork oaks, are making a comeback. In addition, olives, carobs, cypresses, poplars and many shrubs, from spiny broom to asparagus ferns, flourish.

Hiking trails thread the park which shelters weasels, polecats, foxes, badgers, boar and other wild life. Chameleons abound but they are so well-camouflaged you'll be lucky to see one. You may sight kestrels, barn owls, partridge and even short-toed eagles.

Access to the park is simplest via the old Málaga-Granada road. You leave the city of Málaga on the Camino de Colmenar, passing the San Miguel cemetery, and take the C345, following signs for Colmenar and Loja.

The road spirals upwards, at two points running through a tunnel and doing a 360-degree loop to pass over itself. Great views back towards Málaga and the coast.

On weekends a stream of cars flows out of the city, spilling out families at the series of ventas (roadside inns) along the route. Eating out at one of these can be highly entertaining, but only if you enjoy high-decibel conversation, children running in all directions, and gargantuan meals.

A popular dish is the *plato montés*, a plate piled with chips, sausages, eggs, fried peppers, and other ingredients. All of this is washed down with *vino del monte*, Málaga wine from the barrel.

You can't go wrong at most of the inns. Worth trying: Venta Galwey (Ctra de los Montes, km544. Tel. 952 11 01 28), 19 kilometres from Málaga, which specialises in venison and wild boar.

Opposite the ventas El Mijeño and El Boticario (just after the 553km marker), a left turn takes you along a dirt track into the nature park. Sick or rescued animals, including vultures and foxes, are cared for at El Boticario, once a winery, a little way along on the left. Visitors not encouraged but you can see the vultures from the track.

The track continues 10 kilometres to a recreation area and one of the few spots where you can overnight within the park, the Hotel Humaina. Back on the highway, you pass the Fuente de la Reina and climb over the Puerto del León, 960 metres above sea-level.

A turning to the left leads 1.7km down a dirt track to another recreation area and the Lagar de Torrijos. The Lagar is a relic of past glories, an old mill housing an ethnological museum with the equipment used for centuries to produce wine, bread and olive oil.

Opening times are a little complicated: Fridays and weekends, also Thursdays between October and June, 10am-2pm. Best to check by calling 951 04 21 00. Guided nature tours, including lunch at the Lagar, are available. Also weekend courses on such subjects as astronomy, native flowers and mushrooms are held in the park at the Aula de la Naturaleza Las Contadoras (call 952 11 02 55 for information, email: lascontadoras@ wanadoo.es). The building dates from 1780 but was remodelled in 1989.

Apart from Málaga, two municipalities border the park, Casabermeja, which lies on the N331, and Colmenar. Follow the C345 northwards through the park and you reach Colmenar, which is in the Axarquía region.

The Montes de Málaga nature park comes under the Delegación Provincial de Medio Ambiente. The park office is at: Mauricio Moro, 2 - 3rd floor, 29006 Málaga. Tel 951 04 11 69.

Accommodation in the park

Hotel Humaina, Ctra de Colmenar, Paraje el Cerrado, Montes de Málaga. Tel. 952 64 10 25. info@hotelhumaina.es, www.hotelhumaina.es. Small, family-run establishment. Traditional Málaga dishes. Facilities for horse-riding, hiking and cycling.
Cortijo la Reina, Ctra. Málaga-Colmenar, km548.5. Tel. 951 01 40 00. info@hotelcortijolareina.com, www.hotelcortijol areina.com. Luxury, four-star hotel amid trees, extensive grounds, 12km from Málaga. Pool, tennis, mini-golf, hiking routes.

ALONG THE COAST

Heading eastwards from the city of Málaga, you encounter four major resorts along the Costa del Sol Oriental and within the Axarquía: Rincón de la Victoria, Torre del Mar, Torrox-Costa and Nerja. These offer a wide range of accommodation and restaurants and are handy bases for exploring the area inland. Vélez-Málaga, the Axarquía's administrative centre and by far the biggest town, stands a few kilometres from the coast.

RINCÓN DE LA VICTORIA

Population: 34,000

Little more than a fishing village until the 1960s, Rincón has developed into a modern municipality. Scores of apartment blocks and hundreds of houses have been built as it has grown into a dormitory town for the city of Málaga, only a few minutes away. But its beaches and seafront restaurants also attract tourists.

Once a railway line from Málaga to Vélez-Málaga passed this way. Now the route has become a pleasant promenade. You can walk from La Cala del Moral to Rincón and Torre de Benagalbón. Near a tunnel at the western end of Rincón the much-venerated Virgen del Carmen sits in a rock grotto, fresh flowers laid before her.

In the square outside Rincón's grandiose, pillared town hall (Casa Consistorial) a stone sculpture pays tribute to Noctiluca, Mediterranean "goddess of fecundity, life and death". It is claimed that the Cueva del Tesoro was a prehistoric sanctuary of Noctiluca.

Don't miss the Día del Boquerón, when thousands of kilos of grilled anchovies are served along the seafront and the end of the summer season is celebrated in style.

Benagalbón, just inland, has virtually been absorbed by Rincón. Little reason to visit unless you are a connoisseur of King Concrete, as the valley and hills have been converted into building sites. It does have a Museo de

Rincón de la Victoria

Artes Populares, displaying typical crafts and agricultural tools (closed Mon, for opening times inquire at Rincón tourist office).

At Valle-Niza, just east of Benajarafe, stand the massive ramparts of the Castillo del Marqués. Built in the 18th-century, it was originally occupied by *carabineros*, a type of border guard. In the Civil War it was used as a prison and later it became a Civil Guard post. The totally renovated interior houses a school for students of catering and hotel management. Once a week they serve meals to the public (see Where to eat). Near the fortress is an ancient quarry, now converted into a *museo de piedra* (museum of stone) with guided visits (check with Torre del Mar tourism office).

BUILT ON SAND

While the sands along the beaches of the Axarquía don't exactly resemble the powdery white stuff found in tropical paradises, they are sufficiently attractive to lure thousands of visitors.

The colour varies from darkish yellow to grey and the texture from coarse to gritty. The colour changes as you head east. Beyond Nerja and along the Costa Tropical in Granada province the beaches mainly consist of grey sand or pebbles.

Every year Málaga's beaches are cleaned and groomed ready for the summer avalanche. Unfortunately, almost every winter winds lash the coast and thousands of tons of sand are washed away — the 2007 storms were some of the worst in this respect.

Thus, every year the beaches have to be "regenerated", a laborious and costly business. Sand is pumped up from the sea-bed, dredged from rivers and ports and even dug out from reservoirs with low water levels. Then it is spread over the beaches.

Nearly 700,000 cubic metres of sand have to be shifted in Málaga province and 100,000 of these are destined annually for the Axarquía beaches, chiefly at Nerja, Torrox, Algarrobo, Chilches and Mezquitilla.

Sights

Casa Fuerte de Bezmiliana. Rincón's most impressive building, an 18th-century military fort constructed by King Carlos III to defend the area against British and Dutch pirates. Now a cultural exhibition centre.

Cueva del Tesoro. Off N340 between Rincón and Cala del Moral. Claimed to be Europe's only marine cave that can be visited. Prehistoric animal paintings and Neolithic ceramics have been found. According to legend, a Moorish king, Tasufin, hid treasure here in the 12th- century. To date all efforts to locate it have failed. Guided visits, 10.45 to 13.00, 16.45 to 17.15 (later in summer). The cave forms part of the Parque Arqueológico del Mediterráneo (open 10.00 to 19.00 (to 22.00 in summer), which includes a replica of a cave wall painting.

Fiestas: July 16, Puerta de la Axarquía Sea Festival, sea processions of Virgen del Carmen at Rincón and Cala del Moral; early September, Día del Boquerón Victoriano.

Tourist office: Town hall (side entrance). Tel. 952 40 77 68. turismo@rincondelavictoria.es, www.rincondelavictoria.com. Open Mon-Fri 9.00-14.00, in summer also evenings and Sat am.

From Rincón to Torre del Mar the old highway, the N340, dawdles its way along the coast, passing former fishing hamlets, Torre de Benagalbón, Benajarafe and Almayate. Developers are busy filling in the gaps so that this section is almost a continuous strip of apartments and chalets, with an occasional field or fisherman's cottage surviving.

TORRE DEL MAR

Population: 15,000

Until the 1960s this was little more than a huddle of fishermen's dwellings on a dusty, gritty beach. Sugar cane extended in all directions. Then a local entrepreneur known as Toto started building apartment blocks. Finding they sold to sun-hungry Germans faster than foaming tankards at the Munich beer festival he built another, and another, and another.

Green spaces, paved roads and other boring amenities did not figure in early "plans". But Torre finally cleaned up its act. The long beach has been improved by a fine promenade, trees have been planted, services provided. The town has grown into a modern resort with numerous shops and

Torre del Mar lighthouse

restaurants, visited in summer by more than 100,000 holidaymakers.

The beachfront is a good place to stroll and enjoy a snack as it is lined with ice-cream parlours and eateries serving everything from pizzas to fresh seafood. On weekend nights the eastern end becomes lively as teenagers crowd the many bars.

For some of the best pastries on the Costa, call in at the Don Pedro café on the main thoroughfare (Avda. Andalucía, Urb. Pueblo Rocío BL.1), just opposite the Comisaría, the police office where non-Spaniards apply for residence and work permits.

Development now extends to Caleta de Vélez, a fishing and pleasure port, and far inland. Vélez-Málaga, six kilometres away inland, has resolutely fought off attempts by the upstart resort to become a separate municipality. Not unconnected with this conflict is the inauguration in 2006 of a costly tram service linking Vélez-Málaga with Torre del Mar.

The Parque de la Memoria commemorates those who died when thousands fled along the road to Almería in 1937 after the fall of Málaga to Nationalist forces (see History's long footprint). A plaque bears the signatures of about 400 survivors.

Torre was once important for sugar cane production and Spain's first industrial-scale factory was established there in 1845. The administration centre was Casa Larios, now a local government office off the Avenida de Andalucía. In front is a large steam engine, built in Lille, France, acquired in 1900 by José Larios for grinding the cane. To the rear of Casa Larios, the old *azucarera* chimney still stands.

The chimney and steam engine are just about the only tourist sights until the Nuestra Señora del Carmen sugar mill has been rehabilitated. It is to house a tourism information centre which will detail the history of the sugar industry. An exhibition hall and an auditorium are included in the plans.

Fiestas: June 24, magic night of San Juan, beach celebration; July 15-17 Veladilla del Carmen, sea procession; second week July, Caleta de Vélez fair; July 22-26, annual fair.
Tourist office: Paseo de Larios, Torre del Mar. Tel. 952 54 11 04. www.ayto-velezmalaga.es turismo@ayto-velezmalaga.es.
Open: 10.00-14.00 (in summer, also evenings).

VÉLEZ-MÁLAGA

Population (including Torre del Mar): 68,000
Altitude: 60 metres

Vélez (as it is known for short) is the capital of the Axarquía and by far the most important town with a municipal area covering more than 150 square kilometres, including 25 kilometres of coast and the communities of Torre del Mar and La Caleta. It also has more sights worth visiting than any of the neighbouring towns.

The Moors knew the strategically placed settlement as Ballix-Malaca. Ibn Battutah, greatest of medieval Arab travellers, praised it as "a beautiful city with a fine mosque and an abundance of fruit trees". Ibn-Battutah was not a person easily impressed as he visited almost every place of interest between Andalusia and China in the 14th-century. Commenting on its figs, he told the story of a Berber from the desert who said: "Don't ask me questions about those figs — just toss a basketful down my throat."

Miguel Cervantes passed this way during his troubled tax-collecting career and remembered the town in his great work *Don Quixote de la Mancha*, where the lines appear: "Thanks be to God, gentlemen, who has brought us to so fine a place! Because, if I am not mistaken, the land we are treading is that of Vélez-Málaga…"

Modern developments, housing estates and light industry, are encroaching on the surrounding fertile *vega*, fast converting Vélez and its once-poor relations Torre del Mar and La Caleta into a conurbation. El Ingenio, a vast shopping mall including bowling alley and cinema (some films in original version), is located between Vélez and Torre, which are now linked by tram.

Vélez has some fine buildings and it's pleasant to wander through the sinuous streets of the old town below the much-restored Moorish castle. Phoenicians, Carthaginians and Romans left traces of their settlements in the area.

Holy Week is celebrated in particularly sumptuous style in this town. Eighteen religious brotherhoods parade through the streets bearing 25 images to the beat of drums and the acclamation of the populace. La Legión, one of Spain's toughest regiments, put on a spectacular display in one procession.

Sights

Castillo: Much-restored 13th-century castle, reached on foot from the Plaza de la Constitución. The Puerta Real pierces the old walls with a viewing point on top. Dominated by the lofty Torre de Homenaje.

Santa María la Mayor. Calle Santa María: Built on site of the main mosque, this 16th-century Gothic-Mudejar church has a fine brick tower and coffered ceiling. May be closed due to restoration.

San Juan Bautista. Plaza de la Constitución: A 16th-century Gothic church restored in neo-classic style. Christ Crucified carving by Pedro de Mena. Open: Mon & Wed-Sat, 12.00-13.00, 17.00-20.00.

Casa de Cervantes. Calle San Francisco: Cervantes, visiting to

Velez-Malaga mural

collect taxes, apparently stayed in this handsome building with a brick-pillared patio and a well in one corner. Open: 8.00-15.00, 16.00-20.30.

Palacio del Marqués de Beniel. Plaza Palacio: A noble, 16th- century building housing historic archives, with a modern annex devoted to the study of political exile in honour of María Zambrano, a distinguished philosopher born in Vélez, who spent many years in exile. Open: Mon-Fri 8.00-21.00.

Convento de Santiago. Plaza San Francisco: Built in 1495 in the old Jewish quarter, but much modified. The Buen Pastor chapel has baroque decor. Open: Mon-Sat 19.30-20.30, Sun 10.30-12.00.

Ermita de Nuestra Señora de los Remedios. Cerro San Cristóbal.
Noted contemporary local artist Evaristo Guerra spent 12 years
painting frescos covering 1,150-square-metres on the walls of
this hill-top chapel, the only one in Spain painted by one artist.
Religious themes, people and scenes of the Axarquía are vividly
depicted, including the image of a youngster delivering bread. It's
a self-portrait — Guerra's father was a baker. Fine view of the
surrounding area. Open: 9.00-13.00, 15.30-18.00. Closed Tues.

Fiestas: March-April, Semana Santa, a week of religious
processions; September 28-October 1, San Miguel fair. Third week
of December, Juan Breva flamenco festival (Breva was a legendary
local singer).
Town hall: Plaza de las Carmelitas. Tel. 952 55 91 00.
www.ayto-velezmalaga.es. Tourism office: see Torre del Mar.

COSTA EXPRESS

One day it will be possible to travel by train along the length of the Costa
del Sol, from Manilva to Torre del Mar and Nerja. That at least is the
dream.

Málaga's metro system, under construction, is planned eventually
to reach Rincón de la Victoria. Already running is a tram line (cost: 25
million euros for the track plus five million euros for each tram, much
of it contributed by generous European taxpayers) between Vélez and
Torre del Mar.

Metro and tram will connect when a track is built on the 18
kilometres between Torre and Rincón. Another tram line would run from
Torre to Nerja. Sooner, or maybe later,

East of Torre del Mar along the N340, mountains loom closer to the
coast. Tourism development proceeds apace so that one settlement hardly
appears distinguishable from the next. At high-rise **Algarrobo-Costa** the
most interesting sight is an old watch tower, now totally surrounded by
apartment blocks.

Tiny **Mezquitilla** has also discovered that sun-worshippers bring
higher returns than trawling for sardines. A monument commemorates
Cervantes's landing at Mezquitilla when he returned from long years of
imprisonment in Algiers — unfortunately this seems to be more legend
than fact.

Near **El Morche** a track winds inland up the Barranco de Huit,
bordered by plastic greenhouses. During the 1940s many inhabitants of
this valley were imprisoned because of their support for the anti-Franco
guerrilla movement.

TORROX-COSTA

High-rise blocks line the beach at this point and inland towards the old town scores of apartment and villa developments march up the hillsides. Germans and British predominate among recent arrivals.

Fortifications once existed on the site of Torrox light-house, but the British and French combined to destroy these during the War of Independence.

Near the light-house the remains have been excavated of a Roman necropolis, ceramic ovens, baths and a villa, named Caviclum. Two thousand years ago a fish factory operated here, producing *garum* — a foul-smelling sauce considered a delicacy by the Romans — which was exported across the Mediterranean.

Tourism office: Centro Internacional Bloque 79 bajo.
Tel. 952 53 02 25. www.Turismotorrox.com,
torrox@turismotorrox.com. Open 9.00-14.00.

TORROX

Population: 15,000
Altitude: 120 metres

"The Very Noble and Very Loyal Town of Torrox" insists it has Europe's best climate (something about which neighbouring Nerja and Torre del Mar may have something to say). The original settlement, typically Moorish in style with its narrow, winding streets, poses picturesquely on a ridge four kilometres inland. But its proximity to the sea has transformed what was once an agricultural town into a booming tourist centre.

Climbing up towards the old town, you pass Las Nieves convent, founded in the 16th-century, and its Mudejar-style chapel. Above the pleasant main square with its pavement cafés stands the 18th-century Encarnación parish church. Several traces remain of the Moorish domination, including the Torreón Arabe, a 12th-century tower, and the Portón, a gateway. One of the greatest Moorish leaders, al-Mansur, was reputedly born in a castle at Torrox in 983.

Luis de Torres, a convert from Judaism who travelled to the New World serving as interpreter to Columbus (which languages he was interpreting is none too clear), lived in one old Torrox building. And the Inquisition held court at the same address. That's what they say… but facts do tend to blur over the centuries.

Torrox is at its liveliest at a fiesta just before Christmas when thousands tuck into *migas*, a typical, belly-filling country dish, served with a certain amount of local Moscatel wine. About 2,000 kilos of flour and 500 litres of oil go into the *migas* cooked in the open air in large paella pans. While the music plays, dancers whirl, songs ring out and the party goes on until late.

Fiestas: May 3, Día de la Cruz; first week October, annual fair; Sunday in mid-December, Día de las Migas.

Town hall: Plaza Constitución, 1. Tel. 952 53 82 00.

NERJA'S RISE TO FAME

Two events put Nerja on the tourist map: the discovery of the Nerja cave and a television series.

In July, 1957, a youngster named Francisco Navas Montesinos decided to explore a crevice in the rock near his home village of Maro. Lowering himself by a rope, he penetrated a large cave. That was as far as it went until January 12, 1959, when he and four other boys took the exploration further and came across vast caverns with amazing rock formations and traces of human habitation.

The discovery hit the headlines and Nerja suddenly acquired one of the country's biggest tourist attractions. General Franco himself came to view this underground phenomenon with traces of Paleolithic man, who resided here 15,000 or more years ago. Today in Andalusia only the Alhambra Palace in Granada draws more visitors.

Archeologists have rated the cave as one of the most important prehistoric finds around the Mediterranean. Their investigations have turned up valuable evidence of primitive man's life style — snakes, rabbits, turtles and shellfish were part of his diet. Tribes of Iberians recorded their hunting prowess on the cave walls.

Visitors are guided about the caves, dubbed with names like the Hall of the Cataclysm and the Hall of the Phantoms, by walkways with vistas of dramatic rock formations created by the steady drip of water over the ages. The cave boasts the world's largest stalactite, 60 metres high and 18 metres in diameter.. Not everybody appreciates the Disneyesque atmosphere created by piped music and theatrical lighting.

Officially opened to the public in 1960 with a performance of the ballet *Swan Lake,* the cave hosts an annual international music and dance festival. Every July audiences (including such notables as Spain's Queen Sofía) file underground to view world-class performers, from cellist Rostropovitch to flamenco dancer Joaquín Cortés and tenor José Carreras. The acoustics are first-class, with extra colour added by an occasional bat flitting past.

If you want to reach parts of the cave the average tourist cannot reach, sign up for a guided tour. Two guides will show you prehistoric wall paintings, strange rock formations and vast chambers in a tour of four or five hours. Helmets with lights, overalls and harness are issued to participants. Strong footwear advised. Those suffering from claustrophobia better not apply.

In the early 1980s Televisión Española put Nerja in the spotlight once more. A series called *Verano Azul* was filmed in the town, relating the holiday adventures of a gang of seven children. It was a big hit and played a significant part in making Nerja a must-visit for millions of Spaniards. Ayo, a colourful creator of giant paellas on Burriana beach, achieved national fame.

So seriously did Spain take the 19-part series that when the character Chanquete, an old fisherman, "died" Nerja town hall flew its flag at half-mast. A street was named after Antonio Ferrándiz, the actor who played the part, and his portrait in oils hangs in the town hall. Chanquete's fishing boat has been preserved in a parking zone named *Verano Azul*. And a monument to the series director, Antonio Mercero, stands on the Burriana beach.

NERJA

Population: 20,000
Altitude: 21 metres

The British took a long time to discover this beautifully located town with its extensive beaches, verdant farmland and backdrop of jagged peaks. But now they seem to have taken it over, far outnumbering other arrivals from northern Europe.

British clubs, pubs and publications are everywhere. Foreigners, mostly British, run one-third of Nerja's businesses, especially bars and real estate offices. So widespread is the use of an alien tongue that the town hall issued an edict insisting that business signs must be in Spanish as well as English.

The earliest record of English visitors to Nerja dates back to 1812, It was during the Spanish War of Independence when Britain allied with Spain against the French. They came aboard timber men o'war and proceeded to bombard and dynamite coastal forts to prevent their use by Napoleon's troops. Left in ruins were the fortifications atop a rocky promontory known to *nerjeños* as "el Balcón", another overlooking the Torrecilla beach and another at Torrox.

The general directing the assault, Lord Blayney, was later captured while besieging the fort at Fuengirola and spent four years as a prisoner of the French.

Some years later a more illustrious visitor turned up. Following the great earthquake of 1884 that wreaked havoc in Granada and Málaga provinces, King Alfonso XII visited and walked out on to the headland at Nerja to admire the view. Impressed at the panorama of beaches, sheltered coves and sheer cliffs tumbling into the glittering Mediterranean, he is said to have commented that this wasn't just any old *balcón*.

"This is the balcony of Europe," he declared (at least so Nerja's public relations scribe of the time reported). The name stuck and today the Balcón de Europa is a focal point for both locals and visitors.

Two ancient cannons, retrieved from the sea, guard the palm-lined promenade, which attracts pram-pushers, voyeurs, idlers, people-spotters and gossipers. Nobody can fail to be impressed by the same view that

Balcón de Europa, Nerja

dazzled Alfonso. And there he still stands (in bronze), gazing out.

More than 1,000 years ago have gone by since ibn-Saadi, a geographer and poet, wrote in lyrical and sensuous terms of his feelings for "Narixa": "Stretched on a carpet of magic colours/While sweet sleep closed my eyes,/ Narixa, my Narixa, sprang from the flowers/To bathe me in all her beauty."

Although the once-humble fishing village is now a fast-growing resort surrounded by urbanisations, Nerja remains one of the Costa del Sol's more charming spots with a somewhat upmarket image. However, attempts to build a local golf course have so far been frustrated (and, more importantly, a long-delayed sewage treatment plant is still on the drawing board — wash out eyes and ears well after bathing).

Stylish modern shops do business along Calle Pintada, the main thoroughfare running inland from the Balcón, but the town retains its core of whitewashed houses and narrow streets.

Nerja's main beach is the busy Burriana, lined with restaurants and souvenir shops. In summer, when Nerja's population increases five-fold or more, this is crowded and parking difficult. But secluded coves are to be found further east, at Maro and beyond.

Nerja has a wide range of restaurants. Also a number of stylish, upmarket establishments, such as La Posada Ibérica (Calle Nueva, 1), serve tasty tapas and a range of good-quality wines.

If you yearn to get away from the main tourist track, tucked away in narrow side streets are such unpretentious bars as La Puntilla (Calle Bolivia) and Los Cuñaos (Calle Herrera Oría), serving drinks and tapas at regular Spanish prices. And nearer the centre is La Piscina (Calle Cruz, 11) — the swimming pool disappeared a long while ago. For chocolate and churros, Las Cuatro Esquinas, at Calle Pintada, 55, is recommended.

Nightlife (particularly for under-25s) is concentrated in and around the Plaza Tutti Frutti and Antonio Millón street, where the numerous bars stay open into the wee small hours.

Sights

Balcón de Europa. Magnificent viewpoint and promenade.

Cueva de Nerja. Ctra de Maro, 4km from Nerja. Information: 952 52 95 20. cuevanerja@vnet.es, www.bd-andalucia.es/cuevanerja.html. One of Andalusia's biggest tourist attractions, near the village of Maro. Open 10.00-14.00, 16.00-18.30 (open until 20.00 in July and August).

El Salvador parish church. Dating from 1697, it is built in Mudejar style, but with baroque additions. Like many churches, it was sacked during the Civil War and the sacred images were burned.

Ermita de Las Angustias. A 17th-century chapel with Granada-style frescos by the maestro Alonso Cano.

Donkey and Animal Rescue Centre. Visitors (and donations) are welcome. Cares for sick animals and finds homes for abandoned donkeys, mules, horses, cats and dogs. Located just off the N340 near some monumental arches as you enter Nerja from the west. Weekdays, 9.30-14.00, weekends 10.00-13.00. Tel. 618 467 575. Postal address: Mail Box 16, Almirante Carranza 49, 29780 Nerja.

Fiestas: February, Carnival; May 15, San Isidro romería; June 16, San Juan; July 16, Virgen del Carmen; second week of October, week-long annual fair. July, International music and dance festival in the Nerja cave.

Tourism office: Puerta del Mar, 2. Tel. 952 52 15 31. turismo@nerja.org, www.nerja.org. Open 10.00-14.00, 16.00-19.00, Sat 10.00-13.30. Closed Sun.

MARO

This hamlet is the last settlement before you reach the Granada border. Perched high above the sea, it is part of the Nerja municipality. A road winds down through farmland to a pleasantly undeveloped beach. In Roman times Maro was known as Detunda. Nearby the Aguila aqueduct leaps a valley. Although it looks old enough to be Moorish, it was actually built in the 19th-century to serve a sugar mill.

FEUDAL HERITAGE

One of the most impressive buildings in Maro is a delightful mansion, known as the Virgen de las Maravillas and secluded amid pines, palms and gardens. For many years it was the summer residence of the Marquesa de Larios. The Marquesa has passed on, but the name of Larios endures, awakening controversy in sleepy Maro because of the feudal situation suffered by hundreds of local *colonos* (tenant farmers).

For generations their families have cultivated plots owned by the Larios company. Rents are low and they no longer have to devote 75 per cent of their holdings to sugar cane to feed the Larios mills. But, because most have no documentary proof of their long tenancy, they can be evicted at short notice. In the battle for recognition of their right to purchase their land at a reasonable price, at one point they staged a sit-in inside the Nerja cave.

Against them is ranged the mighty Larios company, which has multiplied its wealth thanks to the rezoning of coastal land for development (its construction branch is known as Salsa). The courts will decide the issue — one day.

Marine sanctuary

A 12-kilometre stretch of the spectacular coastline east of Nerja, where cliffs up to 75 metres high plunge down to the sea, has been declared the Paraje Natural Acantilados Maro-Cerro Gordo. The aim is to protect the flora and fauna on land and sea in a 1,800-hectare area.

Keep an eye out for wild goats and chameleons. And also for dolphins cruising the coastal waters. Marine life is particularly abundant, with a unique mix of species because waters from Atlantic and Med mix at this point. There are sponges, star and orange coral, anemones, crabs, shrimps, baby squid, sea horses and a variety of fish species. The common finback whale has also been sighted.

Vehicles have been blocked from driving down to the beaches, which are very popular in summer. Visitors can make use of a special transport service to El Cañuelo beach between June and September or walk down tracks and paths. Camping is banned. A virtual exclusion zone exists for two miles offshore where fishing boats and motor craft cannot enter and fishing with rod or scuba gear is forbidden. Heavy fines can be imposed on offenders.

Coast near Maro

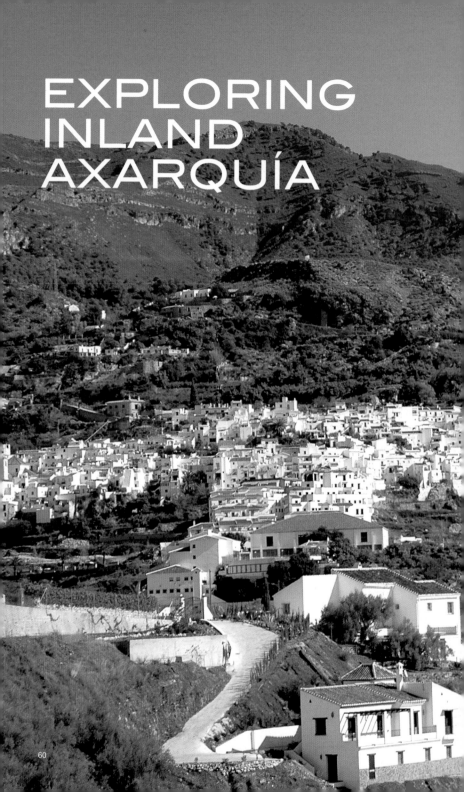

EXPLORING
INLAND
AXARQUÍA

Frigiliana

RESIDENTS of the Axarquía are *axarquicos* and one of the *axarquicos* who has helped to put it on the map is Antonio Jiménez, an imaginative, livewire Vélez-Málaga native. Declaring "this is a privileged region, with great possibilities", in the early 1980s he devised a series of routes to draw the tourists:

ROUTE OF SUN AND AVOCADO:
Rincón de la Victoria, Macharaviaya, Vélez-Málaga, Benamocarra, Iznate, Benamargosa.

ROUTE OF SUN AND WINE:
Algarrobo, Sayalonga, Cómpeta, Canillas de Albaida, Torrox, Nerja, Frigiliana.

MUDEJAR ROUTE:
Arenas, Archez, Salares, Sedella, Canillas de Aceituno.

ROUTE OF THE RAISIN:
Moclinejo, Almáchar, El Borge, Cútar, Comares, Totalán.

ROUTE OF OIL AND MOUNTAINS:
La Viñuela, Alcaucín, Periana, Alfarnatejo, Alfarnate, Colmenar, Riogordo.

You can follow these routes or just wander the many byways — information on the villages is arranged alphabetically.

ALCAUCÍN

Population: 2,000
Altitude: 500 metres

Perched high on a mountainside, Alcaucín used to be as sleepy as any village in the Axarquía. However, in recent years large numbers of non-Spaniards have bought properties in the area so that the municipality, particularly around Puente Don Manuel, is speckled with new urbanisations. Alcaucín's inhabitants are nicknamed *los tiznaos* (the sooty or grimy ones), apparently because in the past many earned a living making charcoal.

The village name has obvious Moorish origins, deriving from al-Cauzín (arches). The attack in 1569 on an Alcaucín inn by the Morisco rebel Andrés el-Xorairán provoked reprisals by the Christians and the eruption of a full-scale war in the Axarquía.

Rosario church, of no great interest, was built in the 18th-century. The village is a useful base for making hiking trips into the Sierra Tejeda. A good time to visit is during the Fiesta de la Castaña, when hundreds of kilos of chestnuts are consumed, along with sweet potatoes.

Alcaucín enjoys fine views towards the Viñuela reservoir, the impressive

Maroma summit and the Boquete de Zafarraya (a narrow gap in the sierra on the Granada border).

Fiestas: May 15, San Isidro romería; first weekend in August, fair, flamenco festival, rock concert; Final evening of October, Fiesta de la Castaña.
Town hall: Plaza de la Constitución, 1. Tel. 952 51 00 02.
alcaucin@sopde.es

CHASED BY SERPENTS

The ruins of Zalía, a Moorish castle conquered by the Christians in 1485, moulder on a hilltop below the Boquete de Zafarraya pass near the Vélez-Málaga to Granada road. Under the Moors Zalía protected the important trade route that ran from the coast to Granada and Córdoba, keeping order and taxing goods.

A Phoenician city allegedly once stood in this area. Some imaginative writers (no doubt after imbibing the local wine) have suggested connections with Ulysses, claiming that here he succumbed to the charms of the nymph Calypso. Another legend asserts that around 400AD, when the Zalía residents refused to accept Christianity, the Lord sent a plague of serpents to chase them out.

Ventas de Zafarraya, north of the pass, was once within Málaga province. Today it and the sister village of Zafarraya prosper because of an unusual geomorphic phenomenon. The adjacent flat plain, totally hemmed in by limestone mountains, acts like a sponge, soaking up the run-off. Abundant water and fertile soil allow intensive crop production. In spring the plain is a mosaic of colour.

ALFARNATE

Population: 1,400
Altitude: 925 metres

Highest and northernmost of the Axarquía villages, lying in the shadow of harsh mountain ranges, Alfarnate has always maintained a fierce rivalry with its smaller neighbour, Alfarnatejo.

Alfarnate's name originates from the Arabic "al-Farnat", meaning flour mill, for the fertile land nearby was once a big producer of grain. Sheer cliff faces and deep gorges form the backdrop — an area of scenic beauty dubbed "the Pyrenees of the South" in a local tourism brochure. A great area for hiking and mountain-biking. A number of paths are signposted.

Alfarnate's parish church is the Santa Ana, 18th century, with a Mudejar-style tower. The chapel of Nuestra Señora de Monsalud dates from the 16th - century.

Near Alfarnate

ANDALUSIA'S OLDEST INN

Because of the two villages' remote position near one of the main routes between Málaga and Granada, banditry was a problem in the past. A favourite rest-stop, for outlaws and travellers, was the Venta de Alfarnate, first opened in 1691 and thus claimed to be the oldest inn in Andalusia.

The inn stands at a lonely crossroads beneath the dark buttress of the Tajo de Gomer. A plaque notes: "In this Venta on April 21 1850 the Mail on the way to Malaga was stolen by a group of 12 armed men. The bandits took particular care to seize a packet of Government prosecutions and criminal lawsuits coming from the Granada chancery."

In another incident, a horseman rode up as the customers were tucking into gazpacho from a common bowl. Told there were no spoons left, he used the crust of a loaf to scoop up the cold soup — then produced a pistol.

"Now," he commanded, "do the same as I do. Eat your spoons!"

Recognising him as El Tempranillo, the most feared *bandolero* of the sierras, they were forced to chew the wooden spoons.

On other occasions, El Tempranillo was more gallant. Always courteous, if he stripped a lady of her best jewellery, he would kiss her hand and assure her: "Such a pretty hand needs no adornment."

These days the biggest risk to diners at the inn is indigestion. At weekends it is crowded with scores tucking into roast kid, partridge and pork.

An unusual fiesta takes place in Alfarnate in February when it celebrates Candlemas. Villagers, especially children, run through the streets dragging burning gorse branches until the village is enveloped in smoke and ashes. Meat is barbecued on bonfires on which scarecrows made from old clothes and straw are ritually burned.

In the second week of September Alfarnate puts on a big show to honour its Virgin — past struggles between Moors and Christians are recalled in a special fiesta, known as La Embajada.

Fiestas: February 2, Candlemas; June 13, San Antonio; September 12 to 15, patron Virgen de Monsalud and La Embajada.
Town hall: Plaza de la Constitución, 1. Tel. 952 75 90 28.
www.alfarnate.org, alfarnate@sopde.es.

ALFARNATEJO

Population: 400
Altitude: 860 metres

Residents of Alfarnatejo, a huddle of whitewash lodged against rocky ramparts near the Río Sabar chasm, are known as "los tejones" (the badgers). The most imposing building is the 18th-century Santo Cristo de Cabrilla church.

Gourmets will be pleased to know that the village is renowned for its *garbanzos*, those chick peas which you boil for hours hoping to reduce their bullet-hard qualities. Perhaps more appetising is the gazpacho which the *tejones* prepare in a special way. Visitors can sample it at the gazpacho fiesta every August.

Fiestas: First weekend in August, Feria del Gazpacho; September, Santo Cristo de Cabrilla fair.
Town hall: Calle Posito, 2. Tel 952 75 92 86. alfarnatejo@sopde.es.

ALGARROBO

Population: 5,700.
Altitude: 86 metres.
Distance from Málaga: 38km.

Nondescript development and plastic greenhouses greet you as you drive inland from Algarrobo-Costa. Down a dirt track on the right, near the Residencia Trayamar, is the Trayamar necropolis. Look for a brick building on the left of the track. Keys to the necropolis can be obtained from the nearby plant nursery, Viveros Velavo, or inquire about access by calling 952 54 73 37.

Phoenician tombs dating from the 7th-century BC were excavated here, but the amphoras and jewellery discovered have been removed to museums.

In the old village of Algarrobo you can take a pleasant wander through the narrow streets, passing the 16th-century Santa Ana church, to reach the San Sebastián hermitage. Built in 1976, this offers good views. Algarrobo's *tortas de aceite* (small cakes made with olive oil) are famous.

The scenery behind the village improves dramatically as the road corkscrews up a steep-sided valley towards Sayalonga and Cómpeta.

> **Fiestas:** Feria de verano, first week of August; Las Candelarias, September 7, bonfire to celebrate harvest and a flamenco night.
> **Town hall:** Calle Antonio Ruíz Rivas, 2. Tel. 952 55 24 77.
> www.algarrobo.es algarrobo@sopde.es

ALMÁCHAR

Population: 1,900
Altitude: 250 metres

The cubist houses of Almáchar, which bills itself as the "Capital of the Moscatel Grape and Garlic Soup", cascade precipitously into a cleft in the hills.

San Mateo church (16th-century), with a Mudejar-style tower, harbours the Christ of the Green Sash, revered for his miraculous powers. He is credited with saving the village when disastrous earthquakes hit in the 19th-century. Fishermen too have had reason to honour him.

Apparently mariners shipwrecked off the coast were saved when Christ attired in a green sash appeared and provided a raft they could use to reach the shore. They searched neighbouring villages to give thanks for their rescue and finally located just such an image in Almáchar.

In Moorish times Almáchar was one of the Cuatro Villas, communities protected and dominated by the lofty settlement of Comares. The other three were Cútar, El Borge and Moclinejo.

For most of the year the village is as quiet as any of its neighbours. But on the first Saturday in September it comes to life. The annual fiesta in honour of *ajoblanco*, a delicious cold soup made from garlic, olive oil and almonds, attracts crowds of visitors. The streets are decorated and in the church square folk groups and flamenco singers entertain visitors until the early hours.

The Museo de la Pasa, which exhibits rustic furnishings and artefacts, shows the process involved in growing vines and producing wine and raisins. You'll find it in a typical village house at number 5, Plaza Santo Cristo (ask at town hall re admission).

Fiestas: first weekend May, Cristo de la Banda Verde; August, fair; first Saturday in September, Fiesta del Ajoblanco.
Town hall: Calle Almería, 14. Tel. 952 51 20 02.
almachar@sopde.es, www.la-axarquia.com/almachar.

ÁRCHEZ

Population: 400
Altitude: 435 metres

A 15-metre-high minaret with ornate brickwork and blind arches testifies to this little village's Moorish past. Built some six centuries ago, the minaret — in a style similar to those found in Tunis — is now the tower of Encarnación church.

Legend has it that during construction a small lizard fell into the plaster and remained embedded there. Any unmarried person of the right age who ascends the minaret's spiral staircase and touches the lizard will be sure to find true love within one year.

Deep in a valley below Canillas de Albaida, Árchez was a prosperous enough place until it was devastated

Árchez-minaret

in the 19th-century by an earthquake, the *phylloxera* plague and disease.

Fiestas: January 17, San Antón, blessing of the animals; August, Encarnación, annual fair.
Town hall: Calle Clara Campoamor, 1. Tel. 952 55 31 59.
archez_admon@sopde.es,
www.consorciosierratejedaalmijara.com.

ARENAS

Population: 1,300
Altitude: 416 metres

A truly sinuous road leads 10 kilometres from Vélez-Málaga to Arenas, but how can you miss visiting a place that calls itself "the chameleons' paradise"? The village claims it has Europe's highest density of these reptiles.

An imaginative former mayor managed to win a few headlines for his village thanks to such clever publicity. More recently, Arenas was in the news when the local priest offended many parishioners by his strictness: he refused to say mass when anyone coughed, blew their nose or cleared their throat.

Every October crowds flock to a newly invented fiesta, the Feria de la Mula. Beasts of burden have been an integral part of Axarquía life for centuries and Arenas was on one of the muleteers' regular routes. In recent years the number of mules and donkeys has fallen sharply, but the fair recalls their heyday and is an excuse for a big party.

The Arenas parish church is built on the site of a 12th-century Moorish structure and boasts an original painting by Evaristo Guerra, an outstanding Vélez artist.

On the other side of the valley a track winds steeply up to the site of the Bentomiz fortress, once a strategic Moorish strongpoint controlling a large chunk of the Axarquía. Ruined walls remain and there are dramatic views in all directions.

Back in the 11th-century, warrior chieftain Abdullah ben-Ziri reported how he took the fortress: "A little later we returned to Bentomiz whose inhabitants, desperate because of their sovereign abandoning them, surrendered. We took control of the place which I put in defensive order. I demolished the fortifications which did not need preserving, I re-estabished tranquillity in the region… and I assured the inhabitants of my benevolence."

Plans are in hand to improve the track and build an interpretation centre on the site. Take a good look around as, legend has it, a great bell of solid gold once hung in the fort. Besieged by the Christian forces, the Moors hid the bell underground and it has never been seen since.

More than one villager, it is rumoured, has sought the treasure with pick and shovel in the dead of night. In vain. But locals say there has never been any serious archeological research in the area.

Fiestas: August 7 and 8, patron saint; October 12, mule fair.
Town hall: Tel. 952 50 90 05.

LA NOCHE MÁGICA

The summer solstice has been associated with strange rites, witches, spirits and magical events since early history and the Axarquía and Costa Tropical have their share.

The hamlet of Daimalos, near Arenas and Vélez-Málaga, marks the solstice by holding a Fiesta Mágica. It revolves around a legend from Moorish times which claims that water from a local spring has supernatural powers. Back in the 12th century, the Moors are said to have used the fountain's waters in fertility rites.

A man who drinks from the Fuente Perdida can restore his sexual ability while a woman can recover her fertility. Any single person who drinks these waters is supposed to marry within one year.

To attract more visitors, the mayor of Arenas invited the unmarried from all over Spain to attend the first Fiesta Mágica in 1994. He also sought to revive an old tradition, known as "la rueda de Santa Catalina". This involves young couples spending the night out in the countryside until dawn's first light. ("Hacer la rueda a alguién" means "to court somebody".)

BENAMARGOSA

Population: 1,600
Altitude: 96 metres

This community apparently grew up around an inn, the Venta Amarga, and was for long known as Gibraltar Chico (Little Gibraltar). The reason: 200 years ago the inhabitants were renowned as smugglers, particularly of tobacco. These days Benamargosa likes to think of itself as the Oasis of the Axarquía. The sheltered environment and benign climate allow tropical fruits to flourish on the fertile lands bordering the Benamargosa river. The Gothic-Mudejar church of Encarnación is the most outstanding monument.

Fiestas: January 20, San Sebastián; April, Fiesta del Campo; first week of June, romería of the Purísima.
Town hall: tel. 952 51 70 02.

BENAMOCARRA

Population: 3,000
Altitude: 130 metres

Moorish origins are clear in this village as in so many others. The name comes from Banu-Mukarran, a Berber tribe. The area was repopulated with

Christian settlers after the war of the Moriscos in 1570. Ceramic plaques relate local history and traditions. Santa Ana parish church, dating from 1505, is Gothic-style with a square Mudejar tower.

The image of Benamocarra's patron saint, el Cristo de la Salud, is credited with amazing powers. On one occasion the saint apparently saved the inhabitants from death in a cholera epidemic.

Music is important in Benamocarra, which claims to have created one of the first bands in Málaga province, early in the 19th-century. Eduardo Ocón Rivas (1833-1901), well-known composer and organist of Málaga cathedral, was born here. In homage to him, the village resounds to music every September, with classical in the parish church, rock, pop and jazz in the Plaza del Calvario and traditional tunas and other groups parading the streets.

> **Fiestas:** Second Saturday in September, Día de la Música, typical dishes served; second to last weekend in October, romería in honour of Santo Cristo de la Salud.
> **Town hall:** Calle Zarzuela, 46. Tel. 952 50 95 34.
> www.ayto-benamocarra.org, benamocarra@sopde.es.

BORGE, EL

Population: 1,000
Altitude: 237 metres

El Borge is noted for three things: its annual fiesta to celebrate the production of raisins, the notorious bandit El Bizco (the one-eyed) and its highly individualistic mayor. You will guess the colour of local politics when you encounter a street named "Che Guevara". Another street is called Calle de las Pesetas in memory of the old currency.

Immense pillars support the three naves of the Mudejar-Renaissance church, Nuestra Señora del Rosario. Its weather-vane has two holes, said to have been made by El Bizco's shotgun. Until he practised his markmanship on the vane, it had never worked, but — the story goes — afterwards it functioned perfectly.

The house where El Bizco, a 19th-century outlaw whose murderous reputation has been just a little romanticised, was born is now an attractive hotel and restaurant, La Posada del Bandolero. You'll find it down sinuous, narrow streets at the bottom end of the village.

There is also a Museo de Artes Populares (tel. 952 51 21 33), at Calle Del Río, 3. It's privately run and only open on weekends and on holidays.

Every September El Borge stages a Día de la Pasa, which attracts

El Borge

thousands of visitors. Raisins are handed out, traditional rural skills are demonstrated and the local wine flows freely to the accompaniment of traditional dances and *verdiales*, typical music of the Montes de Málaga.

Fiestas: May 15, romería de San Isidro; third Sunday in September, Día de la Pasa.
Town hall: Plaza de la Constitución, 1. Tel. 952 51 20 33.
elborge@sopde.es.

CANILLAS DE ACEITUNO

Population: 2,300
Altitude: 650 metres

Canillas perches high up in the Axarquía below the great bulk of Maroma, at 2,068 metres the highest mountain in Málaga province. Look down on rolling hills and the Viñuela reservoir. The whole municipality lies within a nature park and is a good base for mountain excursions, with handy camp grounds. You can start the exhausting walk to the Maroma summit from the village — at least 10 hours there and back.

Canillas was where the Morisco rebellion in the 16th-century started when a man known as El Muezzin inflamed the inhabitants with his oratory. They attacked an Alcaucín inn. After the rising in the Axarquía was crushed, Felipe II ordered the Canillas castle destroyed.

The Gothic-Mudejar parish church of Rosario was built on the site of a mosque. It shelters baroque chapels and sacred images more than 300 years old. Another monument to the past is the Casa de los Diezmos (house of tithes), also known as the House of the Moorish Queen, on the Plaza de la Constitución.

Hordes of visitors arrive in April to celebrate Black Pudding Day. Vast amounts of sausages are consumed along with beer and the local wine. Roast baby goat is a local speciality.

> **Fiestas:** Last Sunday in April, Virgen de la Cabeza and Día de la Morcilla Canillera; May 15, romería of San Isidro; second week in August, fair, flamenco night.
> **Town hall:** Plaza de la Constitución, 22. Tel. 952 51 80 02.
> canaceituno_turismo@sopde.es, www.canillasdeaceituno.org.

CANILLAS DE ALBAIDA

Population: 800
Altitude: 600 metres

Spilling over a ridge on the edge of the Sierra Tejeda-Almijara nature park, Canillas has a beautiful location and is a good base for excursions through the sierras. Fine views from the Ermita Santa Ana at the top of the village, dating from the early 16th-century. It is rated a historic monument. In the labyrinth of streets you come across the Expectación church, constructed in the 16th and 17th-centuries.

Canillas was one of the hotbeds of rebellion when the Moriscos (Moorish converts to Christianity) rose up against their oppressors during the 16th-

CHECK YOUR CHANGE

Although it does not figure in any currency exchange listing, the Axarquía has its own monetary unit: the *axarco*. Notes and coins of copper and silver were issued in the 1980s. They bore the images of a Moorish botanist who introduced lemons to the zone and of Philip II and the Frigiliana mountain which was the scene of an historic battle between Christians and Moriscos.

The currency was the idea of Antonio Gámez Burgos, a local teacher and historian, who was inspired by the fact that El Zagal permitted the region to have its own currency around 1480. Coins called the axarco (face value 100 pesetas), the five *axarquillos* (value 50 pesetas) and the two *axarquillos* were introduced.

This money was accepted in a number of business establishments and you may still see the sign "Se admiten axarcos". Now, however, the coins have become valuable collectors' items. The silver *axarco*, weighing 20 grammes, sells for as much as 100 euros. So if anybody offers you axarcos in your change, accept them gratefully.

century war of Granada. When the revolt was crushed, the settlement's inhabitants were forced into exile.

Fiestas: San Antón, nearest weekend to January 17;
first week of August, fair.
Town hall: Plaza del Generalísimo, 10. Tel. 952 55 30 06.

COLMENAR

Population: 3,400
Altitude: 694 metres

Located on the western edge of the Axarquía adjacent to the Montes de Málaga, Colmenar was long important for its beekeeping industry. Hence its name (a "colmenar" is an apiary and "colmena" is a beehive). It seems that Hamet el-Zuque, the Moorish chieftain in charge of the Comares castle, owned the beehives at the time of the Christian conquest in 1487.

These days pork and its by-products, rather than beekeeping, are big business around Colmenar. Every December, a festival of pork products is held, complete with folk-dancing, considerable wine-sampling and culinary competitions. Thousands of visitors flock in to enjoy free tapas in the bars and consume 1,000 or more litres of wine.

Climb up to the top of the town to enjoy the views over rolling hills. Here you will find a chapel which houses Colmenar's patron saint, Nuestra Señora de la Candelaria. The first structure was built in 1719 by some Canary Island sailors in thanks for their deliverance from a storm. Apparently they were in serious difficulties off the Málaga coast when their prayers to the Virgin were answered (though they would have required exceptional eyesight to glimpse this hilltop from far out to sea).

Fiestas: February 2-3, Virgen de la Candelaria and San Blas;
August, fair; second Sunday in December, Fiesta del Mosto y
la Chacina (Grape Juice and Pork Fiesta).
Town hall: Plaza de España. Tel. 952 73 10 68.

COMARES

Population: 1,500
Altitude: 685 metres

Seen from a distance, Comares is easily mistaken for a snowdrift. The so-called Balcón de la Axarquía is a whitewash vision crowning a mountain-top.

Comares-rooftops

Park on the approach road and walk up to the main plaza. From its lookout point you look over ridges planted with olive trees and vines towards distant sierras, fertile valleys and the Mediterranean coast. At least 12 other villages are said to be visible.

Ceramic footsteps inlaid in the streets lead you about the village. Once the chieftains of Comares dominated a large area and reminders of the Moorish era are everywhere, such as the Calle del Perdón — 30 Moslem families converted to Christianity are said to have been baptised here. Typical Mudejar touches are to be found in Encarnación church, founded 1505. Two towers are all that remain of the Moorish fortress next to the cemetery. These are indeed tombs with a view.

Mazmúllar, a Moorish settlement inhabited 1,000 years ago, stood on a hillside above the Barriada de los Ventorros, three kilometres along the Málaga road. It's a two-kilometre walk up to the ruins. Go carefully as there are subterranean passages.

In July, a primitive form of folk music rings about the labyrinth of streets when a dozen or so *pandas* (groups), with their colourful head-dresses, sing *verdiales* to the accompaniment of guitars, lute, tambourines and violins. One of the three distinctive styles of *verdiales* is named after Comares.

Fiestas: January 14, San Hilario, procession; July, Festival de Verdiales; August, annual fair.
Town hall: Plaza Balcón de la Axarquía. Tel. 952 50 92 33. comares@sopde.es

CÓMPETA

Population: 3,500
Altitude: 630 metres

Spectacularly situated at the foot of the high sierras, Cómpeta is justly famed both for its typical architecture and for its Moscatel wine. When the Moors were ousted from this area, Cómpeta was repopulated by people from elsewhere in Andalusia, including Puente Genil, Estepa, Baena and Lucena.

Wander its narrow, winding streets and you end up in the main square, Plaza Almijara, next to the baroque, 500-year-old parish church, La Asunción, with its distinctive domed, brick tower and Mudejar coffered ceiling.

The illusion that you have penetrated into the "real Spain" may fade here for you are likely to hear more English and Scandinavian tongues than Spanish. Indeed, nearly half the inhabitants come from outside Spain and at the last count there were 32 different nationalities living in the municipality.

Cómpeta

REVOLUTION ON THE LAND

Not so long ago potatoes, sweet potatoes, tomatoes and sugar cane were the commonest crops to be seen along the Málaga and Granada coasts. But a revolution has taken place as farmers have woken up to the potential offered by the mild climate.

Today tropical fruit such as mangos, avocados and custard apples (chirimoyas) flourish in the sheltered valleys of the Axarquía and the Costa Tropical. Hundreds of thousands of kilos are exported to the cold countries of northern Europe.

More than 90 per cent of all Spain's custard apple trees are located on the Costa Tropical. Rich in phosphorus and calcium, the chirimoya has a delicious custardy texture (plus innumerable black pips). Split the fruit in two, add a drop or two of fresh lemon juice and spoon it out.

Chirimoyas once ripe have to be picked and enjoy a limited shelf life compared with avocados which, if prices are low, a farmer can leave on the trees until prices rise. Production methods and marketing have become more sophisticated. Cooperatives embracing hundreds of small farmers keep in touch via computer with prices in Britain or Germany.

The avocado, a nutritious South American fruit credited with having aphrodisiacal properties, was little known in Spain until recently. Now as many as 10 different varieties are cultivated. The favourite, because of its texture and flavour, is the so-called "rugoso", a bumpy-skinned variety.

To an outsider all those trees clothing the landscape look like green gold. But land prices have soared and avocado cultivation requires heavy investment in preparing the land, planting young trees and drip irrigation. It takes about four years before a tree produces any fruit and even then, if the soil is not right or the location is exposed to cold winds, the results can be disappointing.

Avocados have medicinal and cosmetic properties apart from being good to eat, as businessman Pepe Moreno will tell you. He runs a factory at Algarrobo which extracts oil from avocados through a freezing process. This is used in producing cosmetics, as a skin lotion and in cooking. Pepe's product is exported to many European countries.

Oddly enough, the Spaniards eat relatively few avocados. Total consumption within the country works out at an average of one avocado per person per year. In contrast, the French eat about one-and-a-half kilos per person.

Danes were the first of the well-heeled modern invaders to arrive in force about 40 years ago. Since then thousands of other North Europeans in search of a tranquil life style, particularly the British, have flocked in, renovating hundreds of old farmhouses and building villas on the surrounding hills. Dealing in property has become the most lucrative local industry.

You can sample the *vino del terreno* with a tapa in many bars — three of the most popular with locals and new settlers are the Bar Perico and La Casona on the main square and the Taberna de Oscar on the adjacent Plaza Pantaleón Romero. If you're eager for expat company, head out to the Pavo

Real restaurant, at kilometre nine on the Cómpeta-Torrox road, meeting place for Brits (pea soup a speciality).

One of the Axarquía's most popular fiestas is Cómpeta's Noche del Vino when grapes are ritually crushed, the wine flows freely and entertainment goes on until the early hours.

A sign of the times: the old Civil Guard barracks has been converted into the Casa de la Cultura, with a library and art exhibitions. And on an evening before Christmas expatriates and locals listen to English carols while consuming mince pies and mulled wine in the village square.

Fiestas: May 3, Día de la Cruz; several days around July 20-25, annual fair; August 15, Noche del Vino.
Tourist office: Avda. de la Constitución. Tel. 952 55 36 85. turismo@competa.es, www.competa.es.

CORUMBELA

This hamlet on the road between Árchez and Vélez-Málaga lies within the municipality of Sayalonga. You can see Sayalonga across a precipitous-sided valley but to reach it involves a circuitous, tortuous drive.

Corumbela (the name meaning "white dove" is said to be of Roman origin) is little more than a huddle of houses climbing a ridge at 590 metres above sea-level. But it does have one claim to fame: the 13th-century minaret rising alongside the parish church.

Unless you like to test your nerves, do NOT drive into the village. Park the car on the highway and walk the sleepy, narrow streets. From the Plaza San Pedro there are fine views towards the coast.

Fiesta: June 29, San Pedro.
Tourist information: see Sayalonga.

CÚTAR

Population: 640
Altitude: 330 metres

Cútar, spilling precipitously down a ridge, calls itself the "Fuente del Paraíso". Sure enough, on the road into town you can find the Aina Alcaharía spring. A plaque shows a donkey and the message "Alleviate my thirst as I lighten your work!"

The village dates back a thousand years or so when a fortress in the district was destroyed by the Caliph of Córdoba, Abd ar-Rahman III (also written Abderraman), when he crushed the rebellion of Ibn Hafsun. Bloody battles in the 15th-century gave rise to a legend about a Bird of Death. This apparently stands guard over the remains of hundreds of Christians who were pitched into the ravines and tries to lure passers-by to their doom.

In memory of its origins, Cútar holds a Fiesta del Monfí for two days every October. The *monfí* were Moorish outlaws. Many villagers and visitors don Moorish dress for this colourful affair which features falconry demonstrations, traditional dances and Moorish dishes.

Fiesta: August, San Roque; October, Fiesta del Monfí.
Town hall: Calle Fuente, 13. Tel. 952 55 42 47. cutar@sopde.es.

DAIMALOS

This tiny hamlet, 420 metres above sea-level, lies within the boundaries of Arenas and is noted for its wine. The Concepción church is built on the site of a mosque. Some say there's a magical air about the place. Indeed, a "fiesta mágica" is held here. And look for the Fuente Perdida, which is claimed to have supernatural powers (see the box La noche mágica).

FRIGILIANA

Population: 2,700
Altitude: 320 metres

Frigiliana has won prizes as one of Andalusia's best-preserved and beautified villages. And sure enough this village, high on a hillside, has a delightful Casco Antiguo (old quarter) with whitewashed houses and mosaic-cobbled streets.

The downside is that its proximity to the coast — Nerja is just six kilometres away — has brought a deluge of tourist groups, sometimes jamming the narrow byways. Parking is difficult, even with a new five-storey parking area, part of a blizzard of construction which has not added any charm.

Frigiliana residents are nicknamed *los aguanosos*, probably because of the abundance of water or of the juicy apricots once produced locally. Though Phoenicians named a settlement here "Sexifirmio", Frigiliana's name is believed to have Roman origins, possibly deriving from *fraxinus*, or ash tree, and signifying "place of the ash tree".

The foundations of many houses date back to the Moorish era when the intricate system of irrigation serving terraced fields was created. Twelve ceramic plaques dotted about the village recount the epic 1569 battle in which Felipe II's forces crushed the Moriscos (Moors converted to Christianity) when they made a last stand here. Only a few stones remain of the old castle, but a Frigiliana street is named after Hernando El Darra, the Morisco leader.

There are beautiful views from the hill-top above the village, where traces remain of the old castle walls. Beyond, a strenuous walk will take you to the summit of El Fuerte, a 976-metre-high mountain to which the Moriscos retreated. Rather than surrender, women clutching their babies threw themselves over the cliffs.

Three of the four old water-powered mills standing above the entrance to the Casco Antiguo are now private houses. The fourth and biggest is El Ingenio Nuestra Señora del Carmen, which once milled sugar cane and was the residence of the Count of Frigiliana's administrators. Operating since the 16th-century, it houses the last factory in Europe producing molasses — you can buy this *miel de caña* in local shops.

In the Casa de la Cultura, the restored 17th-century Palacio del Apero, you will find a library and an interesting museum showing prehistoric artefacts, including Iberian ceramics, discovered in the area.

San Antonio de Padua parish church, completed in 1676, was designed in Renaissance style by Bernardo de Godoy. It's open to visitors, who can view the religious images and Mudejar-style woodwork.

Several village bars serve good tapas and budget-priced meals. A road beyond Frigiliana soars along lofty ridges (no guard rails) to Torrox, 14 kilometres away. There are magnificent views and several *ventas* offer meals.

> **Fiestas:** January 20, San Sebastián, procession, fireworks; May 3, Cruces de Mayo; May-June, flamenco singing competition; June 13, San Antonio de Padua, romería, fair; third week in August, Tres Culturas festival, concerts, street entertainment.
> **Tourism office:** Casa de la Cultura. Tel. 952 53 31 26. info@frigiliana.org, www.frigiliana.org.

IZNATE

Population: 850
Altitude: 310 metres

Iznate proclaims itself "Paradise of the Moscatel Grape" and to celebrate that it throws a big party every August. The San Gregorio church dates back to 1505, but this is a quiet pueblo with more fiestas than sights. Vines and tropical fruit flourish in the surrounding area.

A curious ritual is re-enacted on the Domingo de Resurrección (Easter Sunday) when the Virgen de los Dolores, shrouded in a white veil, is carried in procession to a local shrine and carefully concealed in an orchard. St. Peter searches vainly for the Virgin and child. Finally he comes across the Virgin and pulls back the veil so she can see Jesus, her resurrected son — at which the celebration explodes, complete with bell-ringing, rockets, gun-shots and a paella.

Fiestas: June 13, San Antonio, fair; August, Día de la Uva Moscatel.
Town hall: Calle Vélez, 20. Tel. 952 50 97 76. iznate@sopde.es.

MACHARAVIAYA

Population: 380
Altitude: 235 metres

Macharaviaya view

Don't be put off by the building frenzy alongside the first two kilometres of the Macharaviaya road after leaving the autoroute. Soon you are corkscrewing over lofty ridges clothed with olive and almond trees until, in a dip in the hills, you encounter somnolent Macharaviaya, small but with a big history.

Two hundred years ago it was known as Little Madrid thanks to the privileges bestowed by the Gálvez family, who became the favourites of King Carlos III and achieved power and wealth in the New World.

The neo-classical San Jacinto church, with a coat of arms topped by a crown above the main entrance, was built with the aid of the Galvéz family. A gloomy pantheon beneath the church is devoted to them, a grey marble tomb honouring José de Gálvez, the most prominent of four brothers.

SAGA OF THE GÁLVEZ FAMILY

For a brief time the little village of Macharaviaya enjoyed amazing prosperity through the good works of a local family, whose members rose to prominence as soldiers and diplomats. Under King Carlos III, they became some of the most powerful men in the New World. They opened up new regions for colonisation and played an important part in the United States' struggle for independence.

José de Gálvez led the way. As an eight-year-old orphan he was helped by the Bishop of Málaga. Brilliant, and ruthless, he became private secretary to the Spanish prime minister and then the Marquis of Sonora and Minister of the Indies.

He played a major role in expelling the Jesuits from Spain's American colonies, crushed a revolt and sent troops and priests to California to block Russian moves and extend Spanish boundaries to San Francisco Bay.

His nephew Bernardo fought the Apache Indians and was named governor of Louisiana. Allying with rebel Americans against the English colonialists (he was a friend of Thomas Jefferson), he played an important part in the American War of Independence. He had a major role in the fall of Pensacola and ejecting the Redcoats from the Gulf of Mexico. The new settlement of Galveston was named after him.

The Gálvez family spent some of their fortune transforming their humble birthplace with paved streets, fountains, a school and agricultural bank. A Macharaviaya factory manufacturing playing cards employed 200 people (the building still exists) — it flourished because it enjoyed the monopoly of card exports to the New World.

With the passing of the Gálvez family, Little Madrid sank back into obscurity. The card factory closed, not surprisingly as demand in the colonies apparently slumped due to the government fixing prices at an exorbitant level.

Macharaviaya's street names — Pensacola, Mobile, New Orleans and La Louisiana park inaugurated in 2006 — recall those past glories. And the village is twinned with Mobile. A United States order known as Los Granaderos de Galves still pays tribute to Bernardo for his help and a bronze statue of him stands in the Capitol in Washington.

Six Murillo paintings are said to have once graced the church and Goya allegedly painted a fresco of his mother on one of the walls. But the building was sacked during the Civil War and no trace remains.

The history of Macharaviaya is recounted in a museum, the Museo de los Gálvez, on Avenida de los Gálvez (usually open Saturday and Sunday mornings, possibly longer in summer). It also features paintings by Robert Harvey, a respected American artist long resident in the village.

Close by is the Taberna El Candil, good for a budget lunch. Take on the locals at dominoes for an extra thrill.

Beyond the village is the hamlet of Benaque, where in 1857 Salvador Rueda, who rose from poverty to achieve fame through his novels, dramatic works and poetry, was born. His birthplace, now a museum, can be visited (call the Macharaviaya town hall to arrange a time).

Fiestas: summer, Semana Cultural, usually held first week of August, during San Bernardo fair; October, Virgen del Rosario, procession.
Town hall: Plaza de la Iglesia. Tel. 952 40 00 26.
www.macharaviaya.es.

Moclinejo

Population: 1,200
Altitude: 430 metres

Standing above the Benagalbón river valley, Moclinejo traditionally lived from the cultivation of its vines to produce raisins and Moscatel wine. It has a study centre for these products with objects used in their preparation. The parish church Nuestra Señora de Gracia, with a Moorish-style bell tower, was built in the 16th and 17th-centuries.

Paella, prizes for achievements in culture, politics and entertainment, fandangos, and imbibing are all part of the annual wine festival which takes place in September.

The most significant event in local history occurred in 1482 when troops of the Antequera governor clashed with Moorish forces of Mulay Hacen in this area and were massacred. Ever since a gully has been known as La Hoya de los Muertos (the pit of the dead).

Fiestas: May, romería, cultural week; September, Fiesta de Viñeros.
Town hall: Plaza de España, 7. Tel. 952 40 05 86.
moclinejo@sopde.es

PERIANA

Population: 3,500
Altitude: 550 metres

South-facing, high up on a mountain slope, Periana enjoys a privileged position with excellent views over the Guaro river valley and La Viñuela reservoir. It is renowned for the quality of its olive oil and for peaches, both of which products are featured in fiestas.

The neo-Mudejar San Isidro Labrador church has an interesting mosaic floor. It was built after a disastrous earthquake which caused havoc in Granada and Málaga provinces in 1884, killing 58 persons in Periana.

The municipality embraces many small hamlets which date from Roman times. They include Guaro, Mondrón and Baños de Vilo. This last was the site of Arab baths. Its sulphurous waters reputedly have curative properties for skin complaints. There are plans to develop a spa.

Fiestas: end of March, Día del Aceite Verdial, celebrating olive oil; May 15, San Isidro; third week in August, Fería del Melocotón.
Town hall: Plaza de Andalucía, 1. Tel. 952 53 60 16.
periana@sopde.es

Periana river

LAST TRAIN TO PERIANA

In days gone by trains trundled along the coast from Málaga to Vélez-Málaga and from there continued into the mountains, zigzagging their way up to the pass at Ventas de Zafarraya (Granada), 945 metres above sea level. The trip took four hours and 25 minutes, goats, mules and other hazards allowing.

All along the route you can still find traces of the line, tunnels, bridges and old stations, some converted into bars, restaurants or homes, others abandoned. Members of the association "for defence of the railways in Málaga" and other nostalgics dream of reopening the line. It would be a herculean task for much of the track has been built over.

Ferrocarriles Suburbanos inaugurated the Málaga-Vélez line in 1908, extending it to Ventas de Zafarraya via La Viñuela and Periana by 1922. The Belgian locomotives took more than two hours to haul the carriages up the steep Viñuela-Ventas section. For years the railway was a lifeline, bringing in farm produce to Málaga, carrying families, black marketeers, servicemen, salesmen to the remoter villages.

It was planned to continue the line all the way to the city of Granada, but it never happened. In 1957 the service between Vélez and Ventas was suspended and 11 years later the whole line closed, killed off by competition from road transport.

The railway would be a great tourist attraction today for it follows a magnificently scenic route and enthusiasts have suggested introducing an electric train on its upper section. Meanwhile, it's a pleasant walk along the old track between Periana and Ventas.

RIOGORDO

Population: 3,000
Altitude: 400 metres

Tucked in a well-watered valley of the Río de la Cueva, Riogordo is famed for El Paso, its Easter Week passion play. More than 500 villagers take part in this event, which is staged over a whole hillside and attracts several thousand spectators. Rehearsals go on all year and the leading parts are much-coveted.

Traces of Phoenician and Roman colonisation are to be found in the area. Queen Isabel and King Fernando set up camp here when they laid siege to Vélez-Málaga in 1487.

Among local personalities who made a mark in history was El Cura de Riogordo (José Antonio Muñoz Sánchez), a priest who took up arms against the troops of Napoleon in the War of Independence and reached the rank of captain.

The Gracia parish church with three aisles dates from the 16th-century but has been much reformed. Perhaps more interesting is the Jesús Nazareno hermitage, founded in 1681. It has a richly decorated baroque chapel.

Stewed snails are a local speciality, served in local bars between May and August. A fiesta in honour of the snail is held at the end of May, complete with large helpings of the molluscs and attendant merrymaking. A cattle fair is held at the same time. The local virgin olive oil and pork products are worth buying.

> **Fiestas:** Good Friday and Easter Saturday, El Paso;
> End of May, Día del Caracol; August 15-20, annual fair, flamenco festival.
> **Town hall:** Plaza de la Constitución, 14. Tel. 952 73 21 54.

SALARES

Population: 190
Altitude: 580 metres

Salares is the smallest municipality in the Axarquía. The pedestrians-only streets climb a steep ridge below the great bulk of the Maroma mountain. Until late last century, only a dirt track connected this hamlet with the outside world.

It was founded by the Romans with the name Salaria Bastitanorum. Although the bridge across the Salares river is sometimes claimed to be

Salares pueblo

Roman, it was actually built by the Moors in the 10th-century. But the big sight here is the Torre Alminar, alongside the Santa Ana church. This minaret with its elegant brickwork was declared a national monument in 1979.

Perhaps you should make a visit to Salares a priority as — although it's been standing 800 years — the minaret has started to lean alarmingly and the mayor has asked for remedial action before the worst happens. Mullahs no longer call the faithful to prayer here, but megaphones installed in the tower announce the arrival each month of the pension payments for the half dozen senior residents.

Salares has one of the best-preserved irrigation systems created by the Moors. It renders homage to its roots every September with the al-Sharq Fair when the clock is turned back five centuries. Concerts by musicians from North Africa, belly-dancing and typical dishes and craftwork give the tiny village the aspect (somewhat romanticised) of a Moorish community.

Fiestas: January 17, San Antón; July, romería of Santa Ana; September, al-Sharq Fair.
Town hall: Tel. 952 50 89 03.

SAYALONGA

Population: 1,500
Altitude: 355 metres

Sayalonga straggles over a ridge jutting into a steep-sided valley and is reached via a tortuous road from the coast. A circular cemetery, an "astounding" alleyway and a fiesta in honour of the loquat (*níspero de Japón*) may detain the curious visitor. The village name, a legacy from Roman times, is said to mean "long tunic".

Sayalonga folklore claims that El Cid, the legendary warrior, visited this village and left the imprint of his hand on a rock. You can find the Fuente del Cid where he slaked his thirst down at the bottom of the village near the municipal swimming pool. If you should also discover the hollow left by his hand, please inform the local tourist office's supernatural department.

The cemetery — actually not so much circular as irregularly oval — was built after King Carlos III, Spain's only progressive monarch in centuries, ordered burial places to be located outside town walls. Its shape is intended, it is said, to avoid the dead turning their backs to one another.

Wander down from the highway to reach Santa Catalina church, built in Mudejar style. Nearby is the tourist information office, which may or may not be open. It is housed in the former village jail. Opposite you find the Callejón de la Alcuza, alleged to be the narrowest thoroughfare in the Axarquía. At its narrowest point it is either 50, 55 or 56 centimetres wide, depending whom you believe. In a region where narrow streets are not exactly in short supply, this phenomenon will surely amaze you — or maybe not.

A Moorish poet, Mohammed al-Hasní, famed for his writings on Mecca and poems in praise of the governors of Málaga, was born near Sayalonga. Appropriately, the village's most recent innovation is a Museo Morisco on Plaza Rafael Alberti (open daily 9.00-14.00, tel. 952 53 50 45). Housed in a building dating back more than five centuries, it is devoted to Moorish culture and architecture in the Axarquía and includes a permanent exhibition by local artist Adolfo Córdoba.

During the *níspero* fiesta more than 1,000 kilos of this fruit are given away to visitors, who are entertained by fandangos de Güi, a traditional local dance.

A pleasant walk from the village will take you to the summit of La Rábita, a 670-metre-high hill offering delightful views towards the coast. On the same hike you can pass by the Ventorrillo de la Aljibe, an ancient crossroads where there are the remains of a Moorish water cistern.

Fiestas: May, Fiesta del Níspero; October 7, romería Virgen del Rosario.
Tourism office: Plaza de la Constitución, 2. Tel. 952 53 52 06. oficinadeturismo@sayalonga.es, www.sayalonga.es.

SEDELLA

Population: 650
Altitude: 690 metres

Sedella's whitewashed dwellings nestle at the foot of the great limestone bulk of the Maroma mountain. Its name is said to have originated with a remark by Queen Isabel la Católica. When reference was made to a battle in the area, she said: "Sé de ella (I know about it)." A likely story.

Sedella was one of the first villages to rise up in the Morisco rebellion of 1569, one of the leaders, Andrés el-Xorairán, being born here.

San Andrés parish church, like many churches in Andalusia built on the site of a mosque, has sculptures dating back to the 17th-century. Near it is the Casa Torreón, with Mudejar decoration, once the residence of a local overlord, known as the Alcalde de los Donceles (literally "the mayor of the young noblemen").

This was one of the first villages visited by the writer Gerald Brenan in the early 1920s when he was seeking a hideaway. Having tramped all the way over the sierras from Granada, he found a poor lodging. There he was served eggs fried in rancid oil and slept in a bed where "I was devoured by an army of bugs till morning. So this was Spain!"

Be assured: that lodging no longer exists and Spain has moved on a little. And rather than smelly eggs you are more likely to be served the local speciality: baby goat cooked in wine.

A visitors' centre offering information on the Sierras Tejeda y Almijara nature park is due to open in Sedella.

Fiestas: January 17, San Antón; first Sunday in August, Nuestra Señora de la Esperanza.
Town hall: Calle Andalucía, 11. Tel. 952 50 88 39.

TOTALÁN

Population: 700
Altitude: 290 metres

Totalán, a humble pueblo located close to Rincón on the coast but hidden in a secluded valley, is proud of the fact that a boy wonder, singer Antonio Molina, spent much of his childhood here — so much so that the first square you come to is named after him.

While Santa Ana church dates from 1505, the Cerro de la Corona dolmen goes back about 2,500 years. This burial place, on a hillside outside town, held the remains of at least 10 persons and pieces of pottery. A steep path leads to it. Archaeologists will find it fascinating, but there's not much to see.

One of Totalán's biggest days of the year comes in November when the driving rhythms of *verdiales* folk music echo through the streets and everybody feasts on *chanfaina*, a hearty stew which includes such ingredients as pork, potatoes, black pudding, bread crumbs, vinegar, garlic, olive oil, cumin and oregano.

If you continue heading inland from Totalán, a winding road up the valley leads to Olías, a humble huddle of houses clinging to a ridge. Park below the village and take a wander. You have the feeling you have fallen off the map, but the many dwellings renovated as weekend hideaways testify that more than a few *malagueños* are in on the secret. Above the village, on the MA133 road to the coast, stands the Ermita del Carmen. One hundred metres further you can park on the left and enjoy a picnic with magnificent views towards Torremolinos and Fuengirola and (on a clear day) Africa. Looking inland, you see the great limestone barrier formed by the Maroma mountain.

Fiesta: Patron saint, last week in May; end of November,
Fiesta de la Chanfaina.
Town hall: Calle Pasionaria. Tel. 952 40 02 15. totalan@sopde.es.

VIÑUELA, LA

Population: 1,700
Altitude: 150 metres

Another "Oasis of the Axarquía". Tucked away in a fold in the mountains, this village owes most of its fame to the nearby Viñuela reservoir. It helps supply the city of Málaga but its turquoise waters have also attracted many newcomers to build houses in the area. In times past La Viñuela village lay on the *camino real* between Vélez-Málaga and Granada, but these days the traffic sweeps past.

By local standards this is a "new" pueblo, only being formally recognised in 1764. It grew up around an inn, which still exists on the main street. It was dubbed "la viñuela" because a small *viña* (vine) grew nearby.

Raisin production has lost some of its importance but the village celebrates an annual Fiesta de la Pasa while the hamlet of Los Romanes, on a hillside above the lake, is renowned for its olive oil.

Fiestas: First week in May, romería; mid-September,
Fiesta de la Pasa.
Town hall: Granada, 13. Tel. 952 51 90 02. lavinuela@sopde.es.

Costa Tropical-sunset

EXPLORING THE COSTA TROPICAL

LA HERRADURA TO MOTRIL

INITIALLY this section of coast was regarded as part of the Costa del Sol Oriental. But, perceiving that they were being sidelined by rival resorts in Málaga province, the folk in Granada province seceded and called their piece the Costa Tropical. Running from the provincial boundary just east of Nerja to Salobreña, this is one of the most scenic stretches to be found anywhere along Spain's Mediterranean coastline. Soaring headlands and cliffs are interspersed with small coves and the steepness of the terrain means that, except around the main settlements, development has yet to make heavy inroads. Between Motril and the sea stretches the flat, fertile delta of the Guadalfeo river, devoted to sugar cane until that industry's demise.

LA HERRADURA

Population: 1,900

Entering Granada province from Málaga, the first settlement encountered is La Herradura, on a beautiful horseshoe bay. It was one of the poorest villages on the coast until tourism arrived. Now it's a pleasant, quiet (except in high season) holiday location, with a selection of hotels and restaurants.

The clear water in nearby coves attracts skin divers. Also naturists — they seek privacy on the Playa de Cantarriján, tucked in below the Cerro Gordo headland, which is crowned by an ancient watch tower.

Back from the beach, between apartments and custard apple orchards, you will find a small castle built during the reign of Carlos III. It is being restored.

On the seafront is a monument in memory of Spain's biggest naval disaster in 1562. Under the command of Don Juan de Mendoza, 28 galleys carrying provisions and the families of soldiers from Málaga to Orán on the African coast took refuge here from a storm. Just when the storm appeared to have passed, it renewed with extreme violence. Trapped between the Cerro Gordo and Punta de la Mona, the ships smashed into each other. Altogether 25 sank and 5,000 people lost their lives.

Andrés Segovia, the great guitarist, was one of those to buy a house in the upmarket development on Punta de la Mona. He agreed to lend his name to an annual classical guitar competition provided it maintained the highest musical standards. It attracts competitors from across the world.

On the eastern side of the Punta de la Mona is the Marina del Este, designed as an upmarket pleasure port. It is picturesque enough, with scores of craft moored, but for some reason life around the port has never taken

La Herradura

off. For most of the year it has a sad, deserted air and restaurants, bars and shops come and go.

Fiestas: March 19, San José, patron saint, fair; June 23, San Juan, night-long beach party.
Tourist office: Tel. 629 069 467. Open 10.00-13.30, 16.00-18.30.

ALMUÑÉCAR

Population 23,000

Squeezed between mountains and sea, Almuñécar is a little offputting at first sight as a wall of modern apartment blocks lines the extensive beaches, San Cristóbal, Puerta del Mar, Fuente de Piedra and Velilla.

But fortunately the old town has been preserved. The attractive labyrinth of narrow streets below the castle ramparts hints at the town's long history. There are more sights worth visiting than virtually anywhere else along the coast east of Málaga.

Unlike many other resorts, Almuñécar retains its Spanish character. While large numbers of north Europeans visit in winter, it attracts mainly

Almuñécar-castle and beach

Spanish tourists in summer. It's a favourite weekend spot for Granada city-dwellers, many of whom have holiday homes here.

Almuñécar is important both for tourism and agriculture. The Río Verde and Río Seco valleys behind the town are a sea of tropical fruit trees. The unique micro-climate allows the growth of all manner of fruit, including mangos, custard apples and avocados. Plans by the town's controversial mayor to uproot many trees to make way for four (repeat four) golf courses with the usual concrete appendages created a furore in 2007.

Almuñécar was one of the first places in Spain visited by the Phoenicians, who established the settlement of Sexi about 2,800 years ago. Excavations have turned up nearly 200 tombs at the Puente de Noy necropolis. The Romans knew Almuñécar as Firmium Iulium Sexi and left impressive remains, including those of an aqueduct and a fish-salting factory.

A bronze statue on the seafront commemorates the arrival here in 755 of Abd ar-Rahman — and the town's Moorish heritage. He was fleeing from the Damascus caliphate where all members of his Umayyad dynasty were being wiped out. He became the Caliph of Córdoba, crushing all opposition.

Almuñécar was the principal port of the Nasrid rulers of the kingdom of Granada and they established a pleasure palace where San Miguel castle stands. During the War of Independence the castle was held by French troops until the English demolished much of it. Another, more peaceful, Brit arrived in 1936 after trekking across Spain, the poet Laurie Lee (see box).

On one of his last visits to the town 60 years later, Lee found just one place where he felt at home as it reminded him of his pre-Civil War experiences. It was the Bodega Francisco, at number 7, Calle Real, in the heart of the old town, where large barrels and hams hanging above the bar give an old-time atmosphere.

You can make a pleasant walk along the seafront and around a headland to the quiet Cotobro bay to the west. With luck you may sight frolicking dolphins.

Night life centres around the pubs in the Plaza Kelibia and Plaza Damasco area. Live flamenco at Taberna El Quejío on Calle Manila. On one or two evenings a week Venta Luciano (tel. 958 63 13 79), 3km from Almuñécar on the Otívar road, puts on a flamenco show and barbecue. It's popular with groups.

In July internationally known musicians play at the annual jazz festival (www.jazzgranada.net/festivales/jazzcosta/jazzcosta.htm). It is usually held in El Majuelo park.

The biggest fiesta day is August 15 when the image of the patron saint, the Virgen de la Antigua, is transported by boat to the accompaniment of a blaze of fireworks as she passes the Peñón del Santo.

SCRAMBLED PASSION

Legend has it that a beautiful Moorish princess living in Almuñécar castle stole the heart of a rich merchant. Her father agreed to her bethrothal only if the merchant could transport a boatful of eggs from Africa without breaking one. He failed and the frustrated lovers — rather than throwing a scrambled egg party — hurled themselves from the castle ramparts, existing ever more as two large rocks in the sea.

Sights

Castillo San Miguel. Built on Moorish ruins over Roman fortifications. Its Mazmorra tower dominates the bay. For years it housed the town cemetery. Restoration work proceeds but you can still visit.

Museo Arqueológico, Cueva de Siete Palacios. Roman galleries house relics from a Phoenician necropolis and a 4,000-year-old amphora, said to have belonged to an Egyptian Pharaoh. Open 10.30-13.30, 16.00-18.30. Closed Sunday pm and Mon.

Encarnación church. Just above the town hall and Plaza de la Constitución. Designed by Juan de Herrera. The tower is the work of Diego de Siloé, one of the architects of Granada cathedral.

Acuario Fauna Mediterránea, Plaza Kuwait. Aquarium inaugurated in 2007. For opening times contact the tourism office.

Parque Botánico Arqueológico El Majuelo. More than 180 species of exotic plants, including a wide range of palm trees and modern sculptures from Syria. Adjacent are the remains of the Roman fish-salting factory. Free entry.

Parque Ornitológico Loro Sexi, Playa de San Cristóbal. Located on a hillside below the castle, this tropical bird park shelters more than 200 species, from peacocks to macaws and ostriches. Open 11.00-14.00, 16.00-18.00 (one hour later in summer).

Peñón del Santo: A lookout point on this rock jutting into the sea offers views of town and beaches.

Roman aqueduct. Several stretches of this impressive old waterway remain, one on Suspiro del Moro road near N340 highway. Particularly impressive at Torrecueva, 3km up the Otívar road.

Colombarium: 2km up the Ctra Suspiro del Moro. A Roman repository for cremated remains. Look for square tower just above the road.

Peña Escrita nature park. Tel. 615 32 14 62. www.pescrita.com Open 8.00-22.00. This 500-hectare menagerie has an unlikely setting, 1,200 metres up in the Sierra Almijara. Animals include bears, camels, hippos, ostriches and wolves. Restaurant, swimming pool and timber cabins. Drive 3km up Otívar road to Torrecuevas where sign on left indicates 11km to the park. Narrow road dips, winds and climbs.

Caliph Abd ar-Rahmán

Fiestas: January 20, San Sebastián, three-day fiesta in Barrio San Sebastián; July 16, Virgen del Carmen, maritime procession; August 15, Virgen de la Antigua, week-long fair, maritime procession; September 29, San Miguel, in district near the castle.

Tourist information: Palacete de La Najarra, Avda de Europa. Tel. 958 63 11 25. ofitur@almunecar.info, www.almunecar.info. Open every day, 10.00-14.00, 17.00-19.30. The tourist office is located in an attractive Moorish-style pavilion built around 1840 by artisans from Tetuán in Morocco.

AS HE WALKED OUT

"The stars snapped shut, the sky bled green, vermilion tides ran over the water, the hills around took on the colour of firebrick, and the great sun drew himself at last raw and dripping from the waves . . ."

That was how English poet Laurie Lee described the arrival of a new day in Almuñécar.

When he trekked across Spain in 1935 — vividly recorded in his book *As I Walked Out One Midsummer Morning* — he came to a halt in "Castillo, a tumbling little village, backed by a bandsaw of mountains and fronted by a strip of grey sand which some hoped would be an attraction for tourists".

Castillo was the name he gave to Almuñécar to protect his Republican friends from rightwing revenge. He found a job in one of the two hotels. The Swiss owner paid him to help in the kitchen, mend doors and play the violin in the evenings.

Almuñécar in those days was desperately poor and he recalls the fishermen toiling at their nets for paltry catches — "a labour without mercy, dignity or reward". When the town was swept up in the turbulence of the

Laurie Lee

Civil War, Laurie and fellow aliens were whisked to safety on a British destroyer.

"There were some grim moments," recalled Lee. "There was the shelling of Motril and I saw two men taken away to be shot in Almuñécar. I saw the dark coming of war."

Returning to Almuñécar in the early 1950s, he found it oppressed and grim, as recorded in another book, *A Rose for Winter.* "The sugarcanes rattled like bones on the wind, and the dark-blue mountains stood close around, sharp and jagged, like a cordon of police."

Although Lee's seductive descriptions of Spain helped attract thousands of tourists to these shores, his name is little known among Spaniards. But Almuñécar has rewarded him with a plaque at Puerta del Mar on the seafront.

Salobreña

SALOBREÑA

Population: 11,000
Altitude: 100 metres

Few towns are as impressive on first sight as Salobreña. Its dazzling white houses, topped by ancient ramparts, clothe a huge rock rising steeply from a flat, fertile delta. At night it resembles a brightly lit ocean liner bulking large against the skyline.

You can understand why Miguel Ruiz del Castillo was inspired to write: "The houses go right up to the sky/like flocks of doves/which have halted their flight…" You'll find these lines on a plaque in the Plaza del Ayuntamiento in the heart of the Albaycín (Granada has one too).

To reach this square, where a history museum is located, and the castle, it's advisable to walk — the labyrinthine streets of Salobreña's old quarter are not meant for motor traffic. La Bóveda, a roofed passage, connects the Albaycín with the old Medina, once the centre of commercial activity.

Local history goes back to Neolithic times, traces having been found in the cave of El Gran Capitán near the hamlet of Lobres. The Phoenicians established a trading post called Selambina. The invaders from Africa arrived in 713 and, under the Nasrids, the fortress became a strategic strongpoint, apart from housing some illustrious prisoners in its dungeons.

The castle has had its share of dramatic moments. In 1408 Yusuf, brother of Muhammad VII, the sultan of Granada, was imprisoned here. One day while he was playing chess with the castle warden, an emissary of the sultan arrived.

Muhammad was dying and wished to make sure that his son rather than his brother inherited the throne so he had sent an assassin to kill Yusuf. When the killer arrived, Yusuf coolly asked if he could finish the chess game, no doubt suspecting evil doings were afoot.

The game was still proceeding when a messenger came galloping up to the castle with the latest news: Muhammad had died and a new ruler of Granada had been proclaimed — Yusuf III.

Between the 15th and 17th centuries the castle was vital in defending the coast against Turkish and Barbary pirates. It has now been extensively restored. Within the walls you can wander through pleasant gardens and view the snows on the distant Sierra Nevada.

The Rosario parish church, a little below the castle, built in 16th-century Mudejar style, has a Moorish-style arch at its entrance with green and gold tilework above. The interior had to be restored after a disastrous fire in 1821. A Christian place of worship was founded here in 305 and was converted into a mosque in 713.

Salobreña has a long sandy beach, split by a large rock which juts into the sea like a basking whale. In summer diners on the terrace of the restaurant perched above the beach, El Peñón, are entertained by daredevil local youths leaping into the sea from the rocks.

During the summer months a large night market operates all along the seafront. During the Rosario fiesta in October a craft fair is held. A craft centre can be visited throughout the year in a building which formerly housed the fish market.

Sights

Castillo Árabe. Open 10.00-13.00, 16.00-19.00, later in summer. Mixture of Moorish and Christian architecture. More than 100 metres above sea level. Fine views.

Museo Histórico, Plaza del Ayuntamiento. Open 10.30-13.00, 15.30-17.30. Summer 10.00-14.00, 18.00-21.00. Human remains, pottery, tools and urns dating back to Neolithic times are on display, plus a photographic record of more recent history.

Fiestas: week of June 24, San Juan; July 16, Virgen del Carmen, maritime procession; first week of October, Virgen del Rosario.
Tourist information office, Plaza Goya. Tel. 958 61 03 14. turismo@ayto-salobrena.org, www.ayto-salobrena.org. Open 9.30-13.30, 16.00-19.00. Closed Sun, Mon.

MOTRIL

Population: 60,000
Altitude: 40 metres

In the 18th and 19th-centuries Motril was known as "Little Cuba" because of the importance of its sugar production. Since the decline of that industry last century Motril, the bustling administrative centre of the Costa Tropical, has opted for tourism.

Modern buildings of no great beauty hem in the old town, graced with a baroque-style Ayuntamiento, dating from 1631. Ask to see the two fine Mudejar coffered ceilings. Nearby is Encarnación church, originally built in Mudejar style, badly damaged in the Civil War when explosives stored there blew up, now restored. Concerts and plays are staged in the charming Teatro Calderón de la Barca, built in 1880 in neo-classical style, destroyed by fire and now fully restored, with ceiling frescoes.

If you walk down the Avenida de Salobreña, you come across a marble monument on the corner of Calle Río Duero, near the Post Office. Look down through a grating and you see water pouring along. You are standing on the Ruta del Agua. This is the Acequia Gorda, the irrigation channel which for centuries has fed the orchards and cane-fields south of the city.

Continue along the Avenida and you reach the Iglesia del Carmen, with a beautiful cupola. This was built to commemorate the 500 victims of a 16th-century plague, who were buried on this spot.

Next to the church is the Parque de los Pueblos de América, which claims to be the most important tropical botanic garden in Europe. It has 36 botanic species imported from the Americas, coconut palms, jacarandas, magnolias…

Above the town — on the hill where Zoraida, mother of Boabdil, the last Moorish king of Granada, once had a fortress-palace — stands a sanctuary to the Virgen de la Cabeza. The Virgin is carried in procession in January when Motril gives thanks for being spared from an earthquake. But the big event is in August when a week-long fair is held in homage to the Virgen de la Cabeza.

Motril has several Chinese restaurants, plus others offering Argentinian, Mexican and Moorish cuisine. You will find interesting tapa bars and eateries on the Avenida de Salobreña. These include Las Tinajas, which features live jazz and flamenco (tel. 958 82 28 97), and La Despensa de la Alpujarra (tel. 958 60 91 35), offering amid rustic décor a large selection of pork products, cheeses and wines.

Formerly, the Guadalfeo delta between Motril and the sea was covered with sugar cane. But now big tourism projects are planned to plant new crops: golf courses, hotels and the usual appendages of mass tourism.

Motril has 20 kilometres of beach, embracing the communities of Torrenueva, Carchuna and Calahonda. The nearest beach to town is the Playa de Poniente, alongside the commercial and fishing port and the yacht harbour, with its quota of apartment blocks and restaurants plus a golf course.

Ornithologists can follow the walkways through the Charca de Suárez, wetlands on the delta of the Guadalfeo river. The 20-hectare protected area shelters more than 160 bird species, including herons, flamingoes and spoonbills, as well as a variety of reptiles and mammals.

Sights

Museo Preindustrial del Azúcar, El Ingenio de la Palma, Avda Marquesa de Esquilache, 4, Motril. Open Mon-Sun, 10.00-13.30, 17.00-20.30. The fascinating story of sugar production in and around Motril.

Centro de Interpretación Caña de Azúcar, Avda de la Constitución (entry at Pueblos de América Park). Tel. 958 82 22 06. Open Mon-Fri 17.00-20.30. All you ever wanted to know about sugar.

Charca de Suárez, Camino del Pelaíllo (opposite Natalio restaurant parking, Playa Poniente). Tel. 958 83 83 92. Open Mon-Sun 17.00-19.00, also Sat & Sun 9.00-13.00. Wetland with many bird species.

Casa de los Bates, N340, km329.5. Tel. 958 34 94 95. info@casadelosbates.com, www.casadelosbates.com. Bates was an English botanist employed by the Catholic Monarchs. A 19th-century mansion is surrounded by 20,000 square metres of gardens, with tropical plants, palms, magnolias, cypresses, waterfalls and fountains. The gardens have been officially declared of artistic value. Charge for entry. Call first, or ring at gate. The turn-off on N340 is more safely approached from the east.

Fiestas: January 13, Día de los Terremotos; August 15, Virgen de la Cabeza, week-long fair; last week October, Semana Verde, agricultural fair.

Tourist office: Avda de la Constitución (entry to Parque Pueblos de América). Tel. 958 82 54 81. www.turismomotril.com, info@turismomotril.com. Open daily, including weekends.

SUGAR CAPITAL

One thousand years of sugar production on the southern coast of Spain came to an end in 2006 when the last azucarera (cane refinery) closed at Salobreña.

Once as many as 29 sugar mills operated along the coast, from Málaga to Adra in Almería province. In its heyday the industry made fortunes for a few and provided work for thousands.

Sugar was produced in India as far back as 3,000 BC. The secrets of its production travelled west and, between the sixth and 10th centuries, the Moors began planting the cane in Spain. They exported this rare product to north Africa and in distant desert encampments the nomads savoured sugar from Andalusia.

When the Christians ousted the Moors, they uprooted other plants and made cane the dominant crop on the coast. Waving fields of cane growing 10 to 20 feet high soon covered large tracts of land. Motril developed into the sugar capital and from its port, Almuñécar and Málaga sugar was shipped all around the Mediterranean and to northern Europe.

Sugar was a highly valued luxury — in 1736 it figured among the wedding gifts of Maria Theresa, later queen of Hungary — and anybody sneaking into the fields to cut a piece of cane to suck was severely punished, with a heavy fine or a beating.

One square metre of land produces 50 kilos of cane, from which eight kilos of unrefined sugar can be obtained. But refining the product took a heavy toll on natural resources. A pre-industrial sugar mill consumed about 3,000 cartloads of timber every season, destroying vast areas of forest.

Columbus took sugar cane to the New World on his second voyage in 1493. It flourished in the Caribbean colonies and their competition, plus the development of an alternative source of sugar (German chemists succeeded in isolating sugar crystals from beet and the first beet-sugar factory began operating in 1802 in Silesia), contributed to a slump late in the 18th century.

However, the introduction of steam-driven machinery brought a new boom in the 19th century. Large mills flourished along the coast, six in Motril alone. The Larios company with its vast landholdings dominated the industry in Málaga province.

Every spring season young men from a wide area trekked to the coastal canefields. Working in teams and paid by the load, they worked long, exhausting hours, cutting the cane and transporting it to the mills.

But in the 1980s the industry went into swift decline. Labour costs rose and the Spanish product could not compete with sugar from other sources. Now the cane-fields are giving way to apartment blocks, villas and golf courses.

One by one the mills along the coast closed. Motril closed its last in 1985. Salobreña finally followed suit in 2006. Rum distilleries closed too. The Motril area was a pioneer in the production of this alcohol, made by distilling molasses. Distilleries began operating soon after the Reconquest and later the Spaniards introduced rum manufacture in the West Indies.

Beneath Motril's tourist information office an interpretation centre offers all manner of details about king sugar. And you can gain a vivid insight into ancient methods of sugar production at the Museo Preindustrial del Azúcar.

This is housed at El Ingenio de la Palma, the site of a sugar mill dating back to the 13th century and named after a Genoese manager. Grinding mills, a huge press, bubbling pans of juice and audiovisual shows give an idea of the process used before the introduction of steam power.

Plans are under way to create a museum of industrial architecture at the Fábrica del Pilar. Founded in 1882, it was the coast's most important mill, a vast complex including refinery, workers' cottages and a grand mansion. The chimney, dating from 1929, was the first in Spain to be built of concrete.

Rum is still being produced in Motril if only on a small scale. The surviving distillery, run by Paco Montero, makes Ron Pálido, highly recommended by the locals. Look for it in stores in the area.

And *miel de caña* (molasses) continues to be canned by El Ingenio in Frigiliana, the last such factory in Europe.

MOTRIL TO LA RÁBITA

East of the Guadalfeo delta on the Almería road the coast becomes less attractive. Stark, treeless mountains tumble into the sea and the beaches are grey and gritty. New farming methods have enhanced local incomes but not the scenery. Every available space, including terraces cut into steep hillsides, has been covered with plastic to allow intensive crop production. The sheltered environment allows all manner of vegetables to flourish year-round and also tropical fruits, from mangos to avocados. It's not a bad area to hide from the world while contemplating the azure sea, but in summer the modern apartment blocks that have erupted in several spots fill up and so do the beaches.

TORRENUEVA

Population: 1,400

A huddle of fishermen's dwellings has grown into a charmless dormitory town for Motril and a tourist resort, popular chiefly with the *granadinos*. Its name derives from the "new" watch tower at the entrance, built in the 18th-century and now surrounded by high-rise apartment blocks. Close by is La Joya beach, bounded by cliffs and miraculously preserved from development.

Fiesta: July 16, Virgen del Carmen.

Carchuna tower

CARCHUNA

Population: 100

From the lighthouse on the headland of Cabo Sacratif you have a study in contrasts — views of the glittering Mediterranean and the glittering sea of plastic behind the Carchuna beach. Wind-surfers love the four-kilometre beach, which runs from Sacratif to a small, leaning tower known as El Farillo (the little light-house).

The only point of interest is a square fortress built in 1783 to keep the Barbary pirates at bay. The massive brick and stone walls stand by the beach, hemmed in by greenhouses.

Here, during the Civil War, a guerrilla group known as Los Niños de la Noche (kids of the night) staged an unprecedented rescue. In the spring of 1938 they freed 300 Republicans, officers and men, held in the Carchuna fort and escorted them through Nationalist territory to the Republican lines, all without firing a shot.

Fiesta: first week July, Virgen de los Llanos; July 16, Virgen del Carmen.

CALAHONDA

Population: 1,000

On its eastern side this village is bounded by a sheer cliff, lending a dramatic air to the place. Snorkellers can find something of interest amid the clear water and rocks below. Modern development has invaded to cater for the beach crowd which flocks in every summer.

Fiesta: end July, Virgen del Carmen and San Joaquín.

CASTELL DE FERRO

Population: 1,300

This settlement was founded in 1760 by Gualchos fishermen. The Castell (castle), now in ruins, was built by the Romans to guard a strategic route into the interior and reconstructed in 1238 by the Moorish king of Granada, ben-Alhamar.

Plastic greenhouses cover every spare centimetre of arable land behind the village, which has grown into a minor tourist resort, with mainly Spanish visitors. Breakwaters protect the beaches. Off-season it should not be difficult to obtain a room at the low-priced one-star Hotel Ibérico (tel. 958 65 60 80) or the pension Costa Sol (tel. 958 65 60 54).

Fiesta: July 16, Virgen del Carmen.
Town hall: Escuelas, s/n. Tel. 958 65 32 67.

Castell de Ferro

GUALCHOS

Population: 600
Altitude: 300 metres

Gualchos is perched high up on the hills to the rear of Castell de Ferro. The latter has developed fast thanks to tourism but Gualchos still slumbers. The two places are linked by an extremely tortuous road.

In the past, the valley between Gualchos and Castell — now intensely-cultivated and covered with plastic greenhouses — was regarded as an arrow pointing at the heart of the Alpujarras because it gave easy access to invaders from the sea.

Despite its lofty position, in the early 1600s Gualchos was seized by pirates and held to ransom. They were only released when a wealthy aristocrat finally paid the ransom money. More recently the villagers suffered another blow. Upstarts from Castell de Ferro stole the town hall, so it now administers the whole municipality.

According to some rival villages Gualchos folk are "fig-splitters", i.e. so mean they would rather cut a fig in two than give a fraction more weight than a customer is paying for. Obviously a calumny — you will find the locals as hospitable as any in Andalusia.

San Miguel, the 16th-century parish church, is the one building of particular note. Behind Gualchos rises the Sierra de Lújar, sheltering the sleepy hamlet of Lújar. Almond trees splash the hills with pink and white in early spring. In Arab times there were plantations of mulberry trees as silk weaving was important.

Fiesta: September 28-30, San Miguel.
Town hall: Plaza de la Constitución. Tel. 958 65 62 37.

CASTILLO DE BAÑOS

The old coast road, pleasantly removed from the thunder of heavy traffic, meanders along from Castell de Ferro to this hamlet. There are remains of a 16th-century fortress. Castillo celebrates San Juan, June 24. Haza del Trigo, a few kilometres inland puts out the flags for Santa Ana, June 25-27. Both these places lie within the municipality of Polopos.

LA MAMOLA

Population: 700

Until recently hardly more than a cluster of poor fishermen's dwellings, La Mamola has acquired a promenade and several beaches by construction of breakwaters. They may be of grey pebbles but that's enough to attract summer vacationers and apartment blocks have sprung up. Result: although it belongs to the municipal area of Polopos, it is nearly twice as large as that village way up in the mountains. However, for most of the year life is delightfully — or stupefyingly (depending on your point of view) — quiet.

> **Fiesta:** August 14-16, Asunción.
> **Town hall:** García Lorca, 1. Tel. 958 82 95 16.

LA RÀBITA

Population: 1,450

Backed by arid, bleak mountains, La Rábita at first sight hardly invites the traveller to linger. However, the seafront has been spruced up and boasts a

handsome promenade bordered by palm trees.

In 1973 La Rábita briefly hit the headlines when a cloudburst sent floodwaters rushing through the town, causing terrible devastation and loss of life. Since then the town has been rebuilt and the riverbed (dry for most of the year) sealed off behind strong walls.

"*Rábitas*" were fortifications built by the Moors as military-religious sanctuaries and the one here, at the back of town, dates from the Nasrid era. Africans were back in residence recently, but not in the role of rulers — they were destitute, illegal immigrants.

Fiestas: May 15, San Isidro; September 8, Virgen del Mar, sea procession, fair.

Town hall: Ayuntamiento de Albuñol, Barranco M. Tel. 958 82 92 06.

Costa Tropical-plasticultura

INLAND FROM THE COSTA TROPICAL

Contraviesa, Alpujarras-snow

A round trip from Almuñécar or Salobreña will take you to a series of villages amid spectacular mountain scenery. The SO2 runs up the Río Verde valley, densely covered with tropical fruit trees, from Almuñécar to Jete and Otívar. Near Jete a minor road climbs up over the hills to reach Itrabo and Molvízar, descending to the N323 in the Guadalfeo valley.

JETE

Population: 760
Altitude: 120 metres

Clinging to the hillside in the Sierra del Chaparral, Jete is sheltered enough to produce abundant tropical fruits, such as custard apples, mangos and avocados. There are Neolithic remains in the area but the village name comes from "Xet", Arabic for river bank.

San Antonio parish church, founded in the 16th century, burned during the Morisco rising, rebuilt, then rebuilt again higher above the river in the 18th century, has works by Alonso de Mena. Adriana, who lives at number 9 just down the street, will show you the church.

If the carving of Christ above the altar has a particularly tortured aspect, it is understandable. After religious images were destroyed during the Civil War, his severed head was found floating down the river. The image was painstakingly restored.

Virgins are not in short supply in Jete. An image of the Virgen del Agua was discovered in the ruins of a Roman aqueduct. It now rests in a grotto off the highway outside town. The Virgen de Bodíjar, carried in procession from the church to a local shrine every April, appeared to a local shepherd.

Fiesta: January 1, Virgen de Bodíjar; last Sunday in April, romería.
Town hall: Ctra, 50. Tel. 958 64 51 01.

OTÍVAR

Population: 1,200
Altitude: 260 metres

A plaque outside the town hall commemorates the courage of "Tío Caridad", a former mayor who stubbornly resisted French invaders during the Napoleonic Wars (see box).

Like the rest of this area, Otívar lived dramatic moments in and after the Civil War. In a 1951 clash with the Civil Guard in the nearby Sierra de Cázulas, four guerrillas were shot and their bodies displayed to the public before being buried in the cemetery in Almuñécar castle.

Things are much quieter today. Take a stroll along sleepy streets, some with names hinting at past plots and passions. How about Calle Beso (kiss street) and Calle Engaño (swindle street)?

Local restaurants are noted for their *morcilla* (black sausage), mountain ham, and chicken cooked with apple. Wash the hearty feasts down with Vino de la Costa.

Fiesta: December 8, Inmaculada Concepción.
Town hall: Avda A. Caridad, 22. Tel. 958 64 50 01.

UNCLE CHARITY

While the Duke of Wellington marched across the peninsula battling Napoleon's troops in what is known as the War of Independence, Spaniards harried the foe by guerrilla warfare. Granada province became a hotbed of rebellion after the French took Granada in 1810 and demanded large sums of cash as well as grain from local communities.

Guerrrilla groups like that led by Juan Fernández Cañas, mayor of Otívar, proved to be a nightmare for the occupying forces. In its first action, 53 badly armed men wreaked havoc against a company of 600. At one time Fernández had more than 400 members under his command.

Although he was noted for his toughness and bravery, the mayor won the hearts of the countryfolk by the generous help he gave to the needy, earning him the name "Tío Caridad" (Uncle Charity).

The French, however, had other names for him. He boasted: "The Frenchman who came within my sights died. The officers and spies, whom I aimed at first, all had to die. It got to the point where the commanders did not want to confront me and many were arrested for this reason..."

Awarded the title of colonel, Tío Caridad provoked a rising all along the coast which was followed by brutal repression on the part of Bonaparte's men. After being badly wounded in an ambush, he took refuge for 45 days in a cave in the Sierra de la Almijara.

The French finally withdrew from Granada in 1812. Otívar's mayor never fully recovered from his wounds and died in Almuñécar three years later.

LENTEGÍ

Population: 330
Altitude: 600 metres

Pinned high on a hillside, Lentegí has clear Moorish origins. It was known as Qazya al-Intisat, meaning "happiness", and the 16th-century church is built on the site of a mosque.

Lentegi-basket maker

Look for the Cueva del Trabuco bar near the Plaza de España and church. It is lodged right under the rock and, sure enough, the décor features a shotgun (trabuco).

There is a Neolithic necropolis in the area, at Los Castillejos, but difficult of access. El Sequero, two kilometres down the road from Lentegí, is a pleasant picnic spot with barbecues.

Lentegí is located in the Sierra del Chaparral, a spectacularly wild area of cliffs and chasms. The main road — appropriately named the Carretera de la Cabra — corkscrews up to the Mirador de la Cabra Montés, 13 kilometres from Otívar, a great spot to view the coast far below.

Further up the highway (A4050), near the km33 mark, a track weaves down to the Río Verde gorge. This truly spectacular area of sheer cliffs and waterfalls is a favourite with practitioners of *barranquismo* (canyoning). It's also a splendid area for hiking.

Stay on the highway if you are heading for Granada. The road constitutes an amazing feat of engineering as it cuts across a cliff face before reaching a plateau and eventually joining the main Motril-Granada road at the Suspiro del Moro.

Fiestas: first week of August, fair; December 25-27, Virgen del Rosario and San José.
Town hall: Plaza Granada, 16. Tel. 958 64 52 36.

ITRABO

Population: 1,100
Altitude: 390 metres

Sheltered by the Sierra del Chaparral, this little village offers some pleasant mountain walks. A stroll through pine woods brings you to the Nacimiento

Horsemen above Itrabo

(spring) and a waterfall known as the Catarata del Paraíso. The most notable structures are the 500-year-old Carmen church and a 17th-century hermitage, Nuestra Señora de la Salud.

Itrabo is proud of its wine, made from Moscatel grapes, and celebrates it with an annual fiesta. Plastic greenhouses are encroaching on surrounding hillsides and the construction boom has reached here too — British and Norwegian predominate among the new arrivals. Vicente in the Bar Medina (Avda Salobreña) serves local wine and good tapas.

> **Fiesta:** first Sunday in April, Fiesta del Vino; last week August, Virgen de la Salud.
> **Town hall:** Carmen, 1. Tel. 958 62 10 06.

MOLVÍZAR

Population: 2,800
Altitude: 240 metres

Molvízar lies down the valley from Itrabo and a few kilometres from the N323. Avocados and custard apples flourish on the slopes around this village, which has twice won a provincial prize for its programme of embellishment. But that was long ago — in 1968 and 1975 — and modern construction has hardly improved matters aesthetically.

Molvízar is particularly noted for its Moscatel wine. The wine-making tradition goes back some 2,000 years as traces have been found of a Roman winery. Santa Ana parish church was built in the late 18th century.

Fiesta: July 25-26, Santa Ana, Moors v Christians.
Town hall: Queipo de Llano, s/n. Tel. 958 62 60 36.

VÉLEZ DE BENAUDALLA

Population: 3,000
Altitude: 70 metres

Bounded by the sierras of Lújar and Guájares, Vélez perches above the main Motril-Granada highway (the N323), which runs through the Guadalfeo river gorge. Cliffs rise 300 metres from the bottom of this impressive chasm. The village is most easily approached via the N323, although a tortuous back road, the A4133, runs from Motril.

A 15th-century fortress with a tower with seven irregular sides recalls past strategic importance. The 18th-century church was designed by Ventura Rodríguez.

Vélez's name can be translated as "Valley of the sons of Allah" and the fountains and greenery of the Jardín Nazarí are a legacy of the kingdom of Granada. The garden has a complex system of water channels fed by an ancient irrigation system. Jasmine, roses, acacias, palm trees and other vegetation lend colour and fragrance to the garden. (To visit, call beforehand 607 527 556.)

If you are interested in olive oil production, stop by the Museo del Aceite, on the N323, km186.5, which has an antique olive press plus a variety of oils, wines and hams for sale (tel. 958 62 80 48, www.museoidel-aceiteandaluz.com). It is closed on Sundays.

North of the village, by the N323, is the Presa de Rules, a dam on the Guadalfeo river intended to solve the coast's water problems. With a capacity of 188 cubic hectometres, the reservoir behind the dam will guarante — when full — water for agricultural and domestic use for up to 300,000 people.

Fiestas: June 12-15, San Antonio de Padua, Moors v Christians.
Town hall: Plaza de la Constitución. Tel. 958 65 80 11.

Los Guajares

Los Guájares

These three small villages, on a side road off the N323, are wedged in the hollows between the sierras of Chaparral and Guájares. The name Guájar apparently derives from the Arabic "gua-run", meaning abrupt and of difficult access. Which proves to be appropriate enough.

Possibly those who suffer from car sickness should desist for the road consists of endless curves. But the journey is worthwhile as the area is wild and scenic. Guájar Fondón is the lowest village, Guájar Faragüit is the "capital", and Guájar Alto is — surprise! — the highest and smallest. Total population: around 1,500.

The villages were founded by the Moors and the irrigation system built by the Almohads is still up and running. Tropical fruit flourishes on the sheltered, irrigated terraces while almond and olive trees clothe upper slopes.

Guájar Alto's Encarnación church, rebuilt after the 1884 earthquake, shelters an 18th-century image of the Virgin. The village has several bars serving tapas and *choto con papas a lo pobre* (kid with fried potatoes) is a local speciality.

Hikers can find plenty of scope in the adjacent sierras, dotted with pines and mastic trees and the home of boar, wild goats and eagles. From Guájar Alto you can hike up the steep-sided valley of the Río de la Toba along a trail that leads all the way (15km) to Albuñuelas. Towering high above is Tajo Fuerte, a pinnacle where traces of Moorish fortifications exist. A desperate battle was fought on those heights when the Christians ousted more than 1,000 entrenched Moriscos during the 16th-century war.

A tortuous but delightfully scenic road runs from Guájar Faragüit to Restábal in the Lecrín valley.

Fiestas: January, San Antón; August, Virgen de la Aurora and San Lorenzo.
Town hall: Dr Alcántara, 31, Guájar Faragüit. Tel. 958 62 90 53.

CONTRAVIESA

Like a massive stranded whale, this bleak, largely uninhabited range lies between the Alpujarras and the sea, east of Motril. From its upper levels, rising as high as 1,800 metres, you look across the deep Guadalfeo valley to the villages dotting the Alpujarras and the Sierra Nevada. The panorama is particularly spectacular in January and February when the almond blossom contrasts with the distant snow-capped mountains. Vines, almond and fig trees struggle to survive on the high, unwatered plateau, with pockets of human habitation in deep, eroded clefts. The farms are constructed in typical Berber style, i.e. with stone walls and flat roofs of slate and rubble.

Contraviesa, Alpujarrras, Sierra Nevada

ALBONDÓN

Population: 1,000
Altitude: 895 metres

Perched high on the Contraviesa mountain, Albondón has long been important for its grapes and raisins and formerly exported them through La Mamola and La Rábita. Several bodegas are now upgrading the local wine. The parish church has a carving of the Immaculate Conception attributed to José de Mora.

Drive up from Albondón to the heights of the Contraviesa to appreciate the views. Splintered by chasms and dry river-beds, the range is a place of tremendous vistas and huge skies.

Fiestas: end of August, fiesta in honour of San Luis, king of France, and Moors v Christians.
Town hall: Sagasta, s/n. Tel. 958 82 60 06.

ALBUÑOL

Population: 6,000
Altitude: 250 metres

Located up a dry riverbed, facing a steep hillside clothed in almond trees, Albuñol is a workaday sort of place which has traditionally relied on its production of green beans, wine, raisins and almonds. These days it is looking to sun-hungry tourists, emphasising the attractions of the beaches within the municipality and the possibilities for hikers. But it's hard to get too excited.

Albuñol was once the capital of the Gran Cehel, an important coastal region within the Nasrid kingdom. The 17th-century Rosario parish church was rebuilt in 1833 and the chapel of San Antonio is nearly 400 years old. Signs indicate the birthplace of Isabel Gómez Rodríguez, a venerated nun who founded a religious order.

Not far from Albuñol is the Cueva de los Murciélagos (Bat Cave) where the remains of more than 50 people dating from Neolithic times have been discovered, including a chieftain wearing a golden diadem. Esparto weavings and decorative objects were also found.

Fiestas: March 17, San Patricio; April 25, San Marcos; July, summer fair.
Town hall: Plaza del Ayuntamiento, 1. Tel. 958 82 60 60.
albunol@dipgra.es, www.ayuntamientoalbunol.com.

Contraviesa-bodega oenologist

Bodega tinaja

CONTRAVIESA'S NEW IMAGE

Jugs of a hearty *rosado,* known as the Vino de la Contraviesa, are a traditional part of meals along the coast and in the Alpujarras. The region's wines have never rated much attention from connoisseurs, but that's changing. Half a dozen bodegas are making serious attempts to produce quality vintages by restructuring their vines amd modernising their methods.

One of these is Cuatro Vientos, located in a lonely spot high on the Contraviesa mountain and enjoying stunning vistas. New grape varieties have been planted and trained along espaliers, or trellises, so they are better ventilated and easier to work. The vines thrive in unique conditions, at 1,200 metres and more above sea-level, wafted by breezes from the Sierra Nevada on one side and the Mediterranean on the other.

Some wine is still produced with old grape varieties, including the native Vijiriego, which yields a refreshing white. But the breakthrough has been in quality reds bearing the label Marqués de la Contraviesa. With an alcohol level of 14 per cent, these are being produced with Tempranillo, Garnacha and Ca bernet Sauvignon grapes.

No longer are the grapes crushed by feet but by pneumatically operated presses, from where they pass to stainless steel vats and, for further aging, to barrels of American oak. Cuatro Vientos produces around 100,000 bottles a year and the Contraviesa as a whole up to 1. 5 million.

The company's keen young enologist Francisco Molina Castillo notes: "It's not easy to change this region's image and make yourself known in competition with the big companies. But we're gaining recognition — and winning prizes."

Visitors are welcome at the bodega's wine museum and guided visits with wine-tasting can be arranged. Contact Finca Cuatro Vientos, Carretera de Murtas, km4, Murtas. Tel. 958 34 33 25. bodegacuatrovientos@latinmail.com.

To reach the bodega, take the A345 from Albondón towards Cádiar, then turn east on the Murtas road. The solid stone complex of buildings includes the bodega's own restaurant (see Where to eat).

MURTAS

Population: 800
Altitude: 1,100

Visiting remote little Murtas in the 1920s, Gerald Brenan, remembered it as "a grey village of huddled, flat-roofed houses, the smoke rising perpendicularly from its chimneys". Murtas has modernised since then, but not that much.

The village's parish church, San Miguel, is an unusually large, 200-year-old, neo-classical structure. Bronze Age axes and other artefacts have been found in the area. For breath-taking views hike to the summit of the neighbouring mountain, Cerrajón, 1,515 metres high. The stiff climb through pine woods takes about an hour and a half.

Further east, towards the border with Almería province, lies the hamlet of Turón, about as off the track as one can get. Chewing a tapa of cured ham in a bar, a recent visitor blinked at the labels on the bottles of liquor. Several bore General Franco's image, suggesting that as far as Turón was concerned news of the Caudillo's death had been greatly exaggerated.

The Murtas area is noted for keeping alive the primitive, traditional music of the Alpujarras, *el trovo*. This is a folk poem, in which singers compete with spontaneous, improvised dialogue that can cover everything from philosophy to satire and romance. It is accompanied by castanets, guitar, lute, cymbals and violin, and dancing.

The music, clearly Arab-influenced, comes in two styles: the *morato* and the *malagueño*, which is similar to the *verdiales* (see Fiestas — Olive-pickers' lullaby). You can hear *el trovo* at festivals of traditional Alpujarras music, possibly at Murta's May 3 fiesta of the Santa Cruz or at the annual fiesta of San Miguel on September 29.

Town hall: Plaza de la Iglesia. Tel. 958 85 50 02.

POLOPOS

Population: 1,600 (430 in the village)
Altitude: 780 metres

This attractive little village pegged to the mountain-side rules over a municipality which extends right down to the coast. It includes the budding summer resort of La Mamola.

Polopos

Fiestas: July 30-August 1, Tourist fiesta; August 14-16, Asunción; October 6-8, Virgen del Rosario.
Town hall: Plaza, 1. Tel. 958 83 68 13.

VALLE DE LECRÍN

It's easy to miss the Valley of Happiness (as it was known to the Moors) and many do. The main highway from Motril to Granada sweeps past the Lecrín valley, high on its eastern side, so that the villages appear as mere splashes of white in the distance. Slow down and step off — this is a delightful, slow-paced corner of Granada province.

Altitudes, and therefore the climate, vary tremendously for the valley extends from a bridge over the Ízbor river, about 25 kilometres north of Salobreña, to the lofty pass of El Suspiro del Moro, where Boabdil, the last Moorish ruler of Granada, turned for a final look at the kingdom he had lost.

Seismic movements and erosion have gouged deep ravines and soaring cliffs out of these foothills of the Sierra Nevada. Towering over the valley is the Cerro del Caballo, 3,013 metres high. In winter it is often capped with snow while in the sheltered valley below oranges and lemons flourish. Indeed, one of the best times to visit the valley is in February when the almond trees are in full bloom and orchards are aglow with ripe citrus fruit.

Old ways linger on in the valley. You will encounter herds of goats heading for the mountainsides and an occasional farmer plodding along with his mule. Fiestas like the Day of the Cross on May 3 are observed in many villages.

Under the Moors, agriculture flourished and thousands of mulberry trees provided sustenance for silk worms. The valley fell under the sway of Umar ibn-Hafsun when he rebelled against the Caliph of Córdoba in the 10th century and seized control of large areas of southern Spain. During the long rule of the Nasrids, it was important strategically as it controlled the route between the capital, Granada, and the sea.

Fierce skirmishes and bloody reprisals marked the Morisco rising of 1569, which ended with the ejection of the Moorish inhabitants. But their influence lingers on in the Mudejar style of many parish churches and the remains of ancient fortresses.

For some years the valley's population was falling. But tourism is creating more activity and a surprisingly large number of British — including a smattering of pop stars — have acquired properties. Several hundred live here permanently.

Lecrín valley oranges

The GR7, the long-distance hiking route from Morocco to Turkey, runs through the valley and there are many other hiking possibilities.

You may come across references to El Pinar, El Valle and Villamena. This can be confusing as they don't figure on maps. These are new municipalities formed by small villages grouping together for administrative purposes.

ALBUÑUELAS

Population: 1,100
Altitude: 730 metres

Albuñuelas is one of those places where nothing ever seems to happen, but local history tells a different story.

During the Morisco rebellion it suffered terrible reprisals. The men had their throats cut and more than 1,000 women were sold into slavery. Later it was repopulated with settlers from La Mancha.

An early church was burned and reconstructed but collapsed. It was repaired, only to fall into ruin. Finally, part of a Capuchin convent became El Salvador parish church. It contains a 16th-century, Flemish-style wooden triptych depicting the Passion of Christ. Park in the Plaza de Gracias to visit the church, open for services.

Albuñuelas was one of the worst-hit spots in the 1884 earthquake which caused havoc in Granada and Málaga provinces. It destroyed 362 houses, killed 102 inhabitants and injured 500.

On the Plaza de Gracias is the Taberna Montoro, good for local wine and tapas (the ultra-compact women's toilet could also be listed as a tourist sight). The Bar Careto, close to the entrance to the village, is another possibility.

Inquire there about the Casa de las Conchas. The owner, Francisco, has decorated his house with about two million shells (don't ask who counted them), some from beaches, others fossilised examples found locally, plus 5,000 pumpkins and countless utensils, such as plough shares and pottery.

Don't be surprised if in the narrow village streets you bump into a mule. Or a pop star — there's a British-run recording studio here.

> **Fiesta:** January 20, San Sebastián; August 13-15, Las Angustias.
> **Town hall:** Cno de la Era. Tel. 958 67 43 12.

BÉZNAR

Population: 600
Altitude: 580 metres

Nothing much moves in Béznar — except in September when the valley resounds to volley after volley of gunfire. The villagers are celebrating the rescue of the Eucharist in the 16th-century when it was stolen by dastardly non-believers.

A major battle between the Moriscos and Christian forces under the Marqués de Mondéjar occurred not far from Béznar, at the Puente de Tablete.

Near the 16th-century Gothic-Mudejar church of San Antón in Béznar a sign points the way to the Embalse de Béznar. Nervous drivers should give it a miss. Pray you don't meet another vehicle as the route through orange orchards sealed off behind high walls is dauntingly narrow — and the reservoir is nothing special when you get there.

> **Fiesta:** first or second week of September, Mosqueteros del Santísimo.
> **Town hall:** Avda de Europa, s/n, Mondújar. Tel. 958 79 50 02.

ALL FIRED UP

Take ear-plugs if you attend the annual festivities of the Mosqueteros del Santísimo in Béznar. Fusillade after fusillade from ancient muskets crackles about the village from early morning until late evening on two days in September. The event celebrates an incident which is apparently authenticated by a document dating from 1571 in the Béznar parish archives.

The Moriscos were on the point of rising in rebellion when on December 24, 1568, at a meeting in Béznar Hernando de Válor — better known as Aben Humeya — was elected as their king. A brutal war was about to begin.

When *monfíes* (Moorish outlaws) kidnapped María Trinidad, a Christian woman, and stole the holy sacrament, a young ensign called Martín Alonso organised a rescue squad of 30 Béznar musketeers. They chased the raiders and freed nine prisoners, including María, who carried the Eucharist back to Béznar. The musketeers were given an ecstatic welcome and crowned with flowers.

Don Juan of Austria, leader of the Christian forces, learned of this heroic act and gave a pension to María, rewarding the musketeers with the privilege of escorting the Eucharist.

Ever since the Mosqueteros del Santísimo brotherhood, wearing traditional dress and head-dresses of paper flowers, have guarded the local saint in procession while jubilantly firing their weapons. As some muskets are said to be the original ones used more than 400 years ago which have been passed on from generation to generation, it may be advisable not to stand too close.

CÓNCHAR & COZVÍJAR

Vines, olives and almonds are the products cultivated around the tiny villages of Cónchar and Cozvíjar, which in 1974 created a single municipality, named (confusingly) Villamena. Located at 680 metres and 740 metres above sea level respectively, they have a total population of about 1,000.

Cónchar slumbers in a cleft at the end of a road. It's all action: dogs doze, housewives cluster around grocery delivery vans and the church of San Pedro, with typical square brick tower, stands where it always has since the 17th-century.

Things weren't always this quiet, as when St James the Apostle came visiting. He is said to have passed by in a chariot, the Carro de Santiago, cutting two furrows 300 metres long in the rock. However, you will look in vain for this phenomenon as construction of a large wall has buried the wheel-marks.

Cónchar rarely hits the headlines, but in the 1970s attention was focused on the village when Don Saturnino, the sternly authoritarian village priest, claimed a miracle had occurred. A devout local woman had suffered from tuberculosis for years and could hardly breathe or walk. Then she received

Conchar

visitations by night from the Virgin Mary and Jesus, who declared he would cure her. Sure enough, the next time she visited her doctor he could find no trace of the disease. Her damaged lungs no longer showed even a scar.

Sceptics can say what they like, but several doctors confirmed the finding and the woman was suddenly free of her infirmity. Now in her 80s she lives on in Cónchar, serene of character and looking surprisingly youthful. But she shies from all publicity and has no wish to talk about the "miracle". Don Saturnino has passed on.

At the Fiesta del Mosto, January 6, free wine flows in Cónchar village square, along with cured ham and *remojón de naranja* (a tasty salad of oranges, cod and tomatoes). *Mosto* is normally the term used for unfermented, non-alcoholic grape juice, but what is served here is definitely alcoholic. Other fiestas: July 25, Romería de Santiago; August 15-17, San Roque.

The town hall (tel. 958 78 27 10) is in the larger village of Cozvíjar. A 16th-century chapel stands where the Virgen de la Cabeza is said to have appeared — Cozvíjar celebrates this with a procession on the first Sunday in August.

VINOS IN THE VALLEY

Lecrín is not a name that immediately springs to mind when talking of quality wine. But Bodegas Señorío de Nevada is seeking to change that. Created in 1996, the winery owns 21 hectares of land between Cozvíjar and Cónchar. The slaty soil and the unusual micro-climate make for ideal conditions, it is claimed.

The bodega has planted Syrah, Merlot and Cabernet Sauvignon vines and installed the latest fermentation equipment, along with an array of American and French oak barrels for maturing. And it has called on the advisory services of a Bordeaux wine expert. Result: mellow, mature, prize-winning reds.

An 18-room, four-star hotel is planned at the winery. Meanwhile, the bodega can be visited and the wine sampled, by prior appointment only. Call or email. Señorío de Nevada, Ctra de Cónchar, s/n, Cortijo del Camino Real, Cónchar. Tel. 902 300 028. eventos@bodegassenoriodenevada.com, www.bodegassenoriodenevada.com.

DÚRCAL

Population: 6,550
Altitude: 780 metres

Although it claims to be La Perla del Valle (from the Arabic Dur al-Iqíim), Dúrcal is not the most picturesque of places but it's an important shopping and administrative centre.

And it does have bridges. Set above the deeply eroded valley of the Dúrcal river, it boasts no fewer than five. One of these is known as the Roman bridge but is actually of Moorish origin. The seven-arched Puente de Piedra dates from the 19th-century while two modern spans carry a highway and the autoroute.

Most impressive is the Puente de Lata (literally the Tin Bridge), a 200 metre-long iron structure built in the 19th-century for the tram service that once ran all the way to Granada. It has now been converted into a footbridge.

On one side of the main square is the Inmaculada Concepción parish church, built in the 16th-century in Mudejar style. In the nearby Plaza de los Magnolios, excellent tapas are available at the Mesón La Buhardilla, a

Dúrcal bridge-Lecrín

restaurant specialising in roast lamb and fresh fish.

Alongside the river deep in the valley are several watermills, some converted into lodgings and restaurants. One suggested walk is along the Ruta de los Molinos. Bungee jumpers have been known to throw themselves off the Puente de Lata and canyoning is possible along the Dúrcal gorge and in the Cahorros de Nigüelas.

Two kilometres from the village in a commanding position is the Peñón de los Moros, a rock crowned with a Nasrid fort, complete with cistern and tower. What remains of the fortress looks at first like a prehistoric monolith.

Dúrcal is not exactly famous throughout Spain so, when one of the country's most popular singers decided to change her name and call herself after the town, local folk basked in the reflected glory. She actually lighted upon Durcal by sticking a pin in a map when blindfolded. No matter — Rocío Durcal was made an honorary citizen.

Fiestas: February 3, San Blas, fireworks; May 15, San Isidro; August 31, San Ramón Nonato, cultural week.
Town hall: Plaza de España, 1. Tel. 958 78 00 13.
www.adurcal.com.

ÍZBOR

Population: 300
Altitude: 360 metres

Truly sidelined from the world by work on the new autoroute (the original access is via a tunnel off the N323), stands Ízbor, south of Béznar. The village is little more than a huddle of houses perched above the deep valley of the Ízbor river, formed by the Torrente, Dúrcal and Albuñuelas torrents.

Not much to see here but, if you do visit, park at the village entrance. On no account try to drive to the upper quarter — unless negotiating hairpin bends with gradients of one in two is your idea of fun.

Administratively Ízbor has united with the hamlet of Los Acebuches and the village of Pinos del Valle to form the municipality of El Pinar. Pinos, population around 800, lost half its inhabitants when the *phylloxera* bug wiped out its vines in the 19th-century and is still trying to recover. A three-spouted fountain stands next to the Ermita de San Sebastián in Pinos. This 19th-century church is sadly in need of repair, large cracks running across the façade.

Town hall: Era, s/n, El Pinar (Pinos del Valle). Tel. 958 79 31 01.

LECRÍN

Population: 2,300
Altitude: 700 metres

The municipality of Lecrín was formed in 1967 by uniting several small villages and hamlets, including Acequias, Chite-Talará, Murchas and Mondújar, later to be joined by Béznar. The area was known to the Moors as Iql al-Gasb (the sugar-cane district), because it gave access to the big cane plantations along the coast.

Muley Hacén, one of the last rulers of Granada, and his wife Zoraya died in Lecrín-Mondújar (hard to tell where one village ends and the other begins). His remains are said to have been buried high in the Sierra Nevada on the mountain which bears his name.

Mondújar clusters around the 16th-century San Juan Bautista church, which harbours a neo-classical altar-piece and polychrome wood carvings. The wife of Boabdil, the Nasrid ruler of Granada who surrendered to the Catholic Monarchs in 1492, lived for a while at the Castillo de Morayma. If you want to view the ruins, way above the village, prepare for a trek up a steep path.

Across the Lecrín valley

Fiestas: Dec 6-9, Virgen de la Inmaculada.
Town hall: Chite, 8. Tel. 958 79 50 02.

DANCING TO HIS TUNE

The little village of Chite celebrates the Fiesta de los Santos Inocentes on December 28 with a custom dating back to the 16th century. Dressed in medieval attire, the "mayor" for a day, the head of a religious brotherhood, leads his group of officials on a fund-raising mission.

Any young man who wants a girl to dance with him has to pay fees to the mayor and his men for the privilege. More cash is raised by raffling items donated by local inhabitants. And everybody tucks into a feast amid much revelry.

NIGÜELAS

Population: 1,000
Altitude: 930 metres

Although winters can be much brisker at this altitude than in the sheltered parts of the valley, it doesn't mean the locals move any faster — in fact,

they've been dubbed Los Lentos (the slow ones) by neighbouring villagers. A number of noble mansions date from the 18th and 19th-centuries and the parish church has a typical Mudejar-style entrance.

Traces remain of centuries-old water mills. Worth visiting is a well-preserved olive oil mill with its presses which has been converted into a museum. A track winds up from Nigüelas to the summit of the 3,000-metre-high Cerro del Caballo — it's possible to make it most of the way in a four-wheel-drive. Stunning views from the top.

Fiestas: third Sunday of September, Nuestra Señora de las Angustias.
Town hall: Plaza de la Trinidad.
Tel. 958 77 76 07.

PADUL

Population: 6,400
Altitude: 740 metres

Furthest north of the Lecrín municipalities, Padul is a workaday town with light industry on its outskirts. Its name comes from the Latin *padule*, meaning reservoir. This refers to a nearby lake, which has been drained and converted to farmland where wheat, maize, sugar beet, vegetables and orchards flourish. Peat cut from the subsoil is valued for fertiliser.

Padul was the scene of fierce battles during the final days of the Nasrid kingdom. The neo-classic castle of the Condes de Padul, dating from the 17th-century, has features similar to those of the Carlos V palace within the Alhambra. Santa María la Mayor church, built in the 16th-century with a Mudejar-style entrance, shelters a fine baroque altar piece and polychrome religious carvings.

Fiestas: January 20, San Sebastián, bonfires and firing of shotguns greet the procession; September 23-26, town festival.
Town hall: Ayuntamiento, 7. Tel. 958 79 00 12. www.elpadul.es.

RESTÁBAL

Population: 720
Altitude: 538 metres

Restábal

Restábal is the administrative centre of El Valle, which is formed by Melegís, Restábal and Saleres. The San Cristóbal parish church, dating from the 16th century, is the oldest in the Valle de Lecrín but a disastrous fire in 1965 destroyed its archives.

Locals, known as *restareños*, can point out to you *el algarrobo milenario*, an immense carob tree which is reputedly 1,000 years old. It stands just outside the village on the Camino Real de Motril.

Neighbouring Melegís (650 inhabitants, altitude 550 metres), has its own remarkable tree, an elm said to be 500 years old. It stands near the Mudejar-style church of San Juan Evangelista. Built in 1570, it shelters an image of the Virgin accredited to the school of Alonso Cano and a baroque Jesus on the cross brought from Peru.

A local spring spouts water at 24 degrees C which is reputed to do wonders for your skin — public baths have been built alongside.

Fiestas: May 13, Virgen de Fátima, romería to Cerro del Calvario; July 25-26, Santa Ana. In Melegís, the big fiesta is San Antonio, June 13-14.
Town hall: tel. 958 79 30 03.

Rio Verde cascade

Typical patio in the Axarquía

PRACTICALITIES

GETTING THERE

It's never been easier to get to the Axarquía and the Costa Tropical. And soon it will be even easier and faster.

By 2010, if there are no major holdups, new highways and high-speed trains will have revolutionised communications with the Costa del Sol. A new autoroute will link Málaga with Antequera and the high-speed AVE service — due to be completed by 2008 — will mean train passengers can travel from Málaga to Córdoba in only 55 minutes and to Madrid in two and a half hours.

Transport along the coast is also being transformed. A four-lane autoroute cuts through the Axarquía, the Autovía del Mediterráneo (the A7 or E15). This will eventually link the whole Spanish Mediterranean coast with France and the rest of Europe.

Work proceeds on the Costa Tropical section, one of the most challenging sections because of the extremely mountainous terrain requiring a succession of tunnels and bridges. The 97 kilometres between Nerja and Adra in Almería are rated among the most complex and costly stretches in all Spain. Cost: something over 1,000 million euros.

It is planned to extend a tram service, already operating between Vélez-Málaga and Torre del Mar, to Nerja and Rincón de la Victoria. Also projected is a new road which would ease traffic between the Axarquía and the province of Granada.

At present the A335 follows a route used for centuries by muleteers and horsemen, winding up from Vélez-Málaga to a pass known as the Boquete de Zafarraya. The new road would swing westwards towards Periana and follow sections of an old railway line before reaching the Boquete and the village of Ventas de Zafarraya.

Meanwhile, Málaga's Pablo Picasso Airport is doubling in capacity, with a second runway. Reaching the Lecrín valley and the Costa Tropical has been simplified for British passengers with the inauguration of direct flights between the UK and Granada airport.

WHEN TO COME

Sheltered by high mountain ranges from cold winds, the Axarquía and Costa Tropical enjoys a semi-tropical climate. The sun shines for around 3,000 hours a year. While the crests of the mountains may be snow-capped in winter, day-time temperatures on the coast are usually over 20 degrees C. Night temperatures can be cool but rarely fall to freezing.

There can be considerable variation between the coastal climate and that in the sierras. Villages at higher altitudes are often four or five degrees cooler than those on the coast and have double the rainfall.

July and August are months to avoid, unless your work or school holidays rule otherwise. The coast is crowded, the hotels are fully booked, the weather is at its hottest.

Ideally, visit during spring and early summer or in September and October. These are good times for hiking and other outdoor activities. However, the winter months also offer weeks of magnificent sunny weather. Nights are cool, but days are dazzlingly clear. Bring a range of clothing if you come in winter as there can be bouts of heavy rain.

Popular spots, particularly on the coast, can be crowded any weekend by Granada and Málaga city-dwellers making excursions. Advance bookings are advised in peak holiday periods, particularly July-August and the week from Palm Sunday to Easter Sunday (Easter Monday is not a holiday). This is one of the country's most important holidays when city-dwellers rush to coasts and mountains. Not a good time to drive or seek a room.

Local fiesta dates can vary so check them with tourist offices or town halls. Fiestas are not necessarily the best time to enjoy the sights. Shops, banks and public offices are closed, churches and other monuments difficult to visit. Those local residents not living it up at the fiesta may have gone travelling or are "in the *campo*" and therefore out of touch. Hotels may be fully booked and restaurants crowded. There will be extra traffic on the roads.

Horse and blossom

Mule man

Bear in mind the aptly named *puentes* (bridges). These occur when people take extra days off to convert midweek holidays into very long weekends. Two of the most important: around October 12 (National Day) and around December 6 (Constitution Day) and December 8 (Immaculate Conception).

HOLIDAYS CELEBRATED REGION-WIDE

January 1, Año Nuevo (New Year's Day)
January 6, Día de los Reyes (Epiphany)
February 28, Día de Andalucia (regional autonomy day)
Viernes Santo (Good Friday)
May 1, Fiesta del Trabajo (Labour Day)
May/June, Corpus Christi
August 15, Asunción (Assumption of the Virgin)
October 12, Día del Pilar (National Day)
December 6, Día de la Constitución (Constitution Day)
December 8, La Inmaculada Concepción (Immaculate Conception)
December 25, Navidad (Christmas Day)

WHERE TO STAY

Old travellers' tales were full of the hardships they suffered as they roamed the back areas of southern Spain. It's a different story today. Indeed masochistic types may feel it's all become boringly comfortable. No flea-ridden mattresses, no villainous innkeepers…where's the fun?

The problem now is choosing where to stay when examining the large variety of accommodation on offer. You'll find a complete range along the coast, from budget to luxury. Scores of small hotels in the Axarquía and Granada province offer comfortable accommodation, usually with en suite bathrooms. Only a small selection is listed here. It is no reflection on those places not mentioned.

Inland, the picture has been transformed by the phenomenon known as rural tourism. Suddenly, it appears everybody wants to head for tranquil rustic locations. Some rural hotels, often converted farmhouses, are stylish affairs and include gourmet dining. Small bed and breakfast places abound, often run by expatriates.

In addition, there are many *casas rurales*, converted village houses, farmhouses and mills for rent by families or groups. These can vary from the primitive to luxurious. Inquire at tourist information offices, travel agents and organisations which specialise in this field.

Organisations which can help you make reservations in rural hotels across Andalusia (some may offer discounts) include:

Alojamientos Rurales en Andalucía, www.tierrarural.com;
Rural Andalus, ruralandalus@ruralandalus.es, www.ruralandalus.es;
Red Andaluza de Alojamientos Rurales, www.raar.es;
www.ruralnoches.com; www.antiquanatura.com.
Check the following website for useful links:
www.guiarural.com/Estand/Enlaces/html.

The Junta de Andalucía (the regional government) publishes a useful annual guide to accommodation, including apartments and youth hostels. Note: not all the smaller establishments are included.

For good-value places with particular charm consult *Small Hotels and Inns of Andalucía*, published by Santana Books.

Ratings

A blue plaque outside hotels indicates the official rating, one to five stars. At the bottom end of the market, P stands for pensión or hostal. The larger hotels on the coast are often monopolised by group bookings, not the cosiest places to stay for individual travellers.

Remember: star ratings only take into account the amenities provided, not the quality of the service or atmosphere. An intimate, family-run, one-star place may prove more agreeable than a four-star, jacuzzi-and-satellite-TV, package-tourism venue.

Tourist information offices usually have lists of accommodation available in their area. Advance booking is essential for Easter week and the peak holiday months of July and August.

> ## PRICES
> Prices range from around 30 euros a night for a double at a simple pension to well over 100 euros for classier spots. Breakfast is often included. Most of the hotels mentioned charge 45 to 100 euros per night for a double room. Establishments charging under 45 euros are indicated by "Budget". Those charging more than 100 euros are indicated by***. Expect to pay 20 to 100 per cent more during high season (July-September) and Easter week. It is worth inquiring at travel agencies about special deals, as many discounts are available for larger hotels, including the state-run paradors.

Addresses and telephones
Spanish addresses can be perplexing at first sight. Note the following. Street names are usually written thus C/Real, 25-2a. The "C", which stands for *calle* (street), is often omitted. The number 25 refers to the house or block, "2a" indicates *planta segunda* or second floor. *Bajo* after the house number means ground floor. If the street name is followed by "s/n", it means *sin número* (no number). "Ctra" is short for *carretera* or highway, "Pl" is short for *plaza* (square), and "avda" for *avenida* (avenue). Apdo. 166 indicates Post Office Box 166.

To call Spain from most European countries, first dial 00 then the country code, 34. Within Spain the first two or three digits indicate which province you are calling — Málaga numbers always start with 952 and all numbers in Granada province start with 958.

MONTES DE MÁLAGA ACCOMMODATION

Humaina, Ctra de Colmenar, Paraje el Cerrado, Málaga. Tel. 952 64 10 25. Family-run hotel in tranquil surroundings. Riding, hiking, cycling. Pool.

AXARQUÎA ACCOMMODATION

ALCAUCÍN
Sierra Tejeda, La Fuente, s/n. Tel. 952 51 01 20. Small, modern hotel. Views of mountains and coast.

Conjunto Rural Castillo de Zalía,
A402 Vélez-Alhama, km53.5, Alcaucín. Tel. 695 678 158.
director@castillodezalia conjuntorural.com, www.castillodezaliaconjunto rural.com.
Low-rise apartment complex. Magnificent views. Pool, gardens.

ÁRCHEZ
Posada Mudéjar,
Alamo, 6. Tel. 952 55 31 06. www.posadamesonmudejar.com.
Charming small hostal with restaurant.

BORGE, EL
La Posada del Bandolero.
Tel. 952 51 94 50.
Former olive mill where the bandit El Bizco is said to have been born. Restaurant with local dishes.

El Borge-posada

CANILLAS DE ALBAIDA
Finca El Cerrillo. Tel. 952 03 04 44. info@hotelfinca.com.
Renovated old farmhouse with fine views. British-run.
Popular with art and hiking groups. Pool. ✸✸✸.
Posada La Plaza, La Plaza. Tel. 952 55 48 07.
reception@posada-lazplaza.com, www.posada-laplaza.com
Spanish-British ownership. Pleasant small hotel next to
La Expectación church. Roof terrace. Restaurant opposite serves
excellent meals.

COMARES
El Molino de los Abuelos, Plaza, 2. Tel. 952 50 93 09.
info@molino-abuelos.com, www.molino-abuelos.com.
Small hotel in grand old village house, with modern comforts,
antique furnishings.

CÓMPETA

Balcón de Cómpeta, Calle San Antonio, 75. Tel: 952 55 35 35.
info@hotel-competa.com, www.hotel-competa.com.
Views towards sea. Double rooms, bungalows. Pool, tennis.
Casa La Mina, 5km from Cómpeta, on dirt track off
Cómpeta-Torrox road. Tel. 952 52 37 67, 687 564 525.
www.villasaxarquia.com/casalamina, axarquia@villasaxarquia.com.
High in Sierra Almijara nature park, splendid views. Tennis, pool.
Good base for biking, hiking, riding. Restaurant with regional dishes.

FRIGILIANA

El Caravansar, Callejón de la Ermita. Tel. 952 53 35 86.
info@hospederiaelcaravansar.com, www.hospederiaelcaravansar.com.
Friendly, family-run, comfortable. Budget.
Las Chinas, Plaza Amparo Guerrero, 14. Tel. 952 53 30 73.
Small, friendly hotel. Budget.
La Posada Morisca, Loma de la Cruz. Tel: 952 53 41 51.
info@laposdamorisca.com. Tranquil rural setting. Rustic charm.
Wood stoves. Mediterranean cuisine.
Acebuchal, Casas Rurales. Tel. 650 617901/650 956 033.
info@elacebuchal.es, www.elacebuchal.es. Rustic-style houses in
restored hamlet in secluded valley, 7km from Frigiliana.

Village dogs

MACHARAVIAYA
Molino de Santillán, Ctra de Macharaviaya, km3.
Tel. 952 11 57 80 or 952 40 09 49.
msantillan@spa.es, www.hotel-msantillan.net.
Rustic splendour in stylish converted farmhouse. Organic vegetable garden. ❁❁❁

NERJA
Carabeo, Hernando de Carabeo, 34. Tel. 952 52 54 44.
info@hotelcarabeo.com, www.hotelcarabeo.com.
Boutique hotel, elegantly furnished. Views sea or mountains.
Parador, Almuñécar, 8. Tel. 952 52 00 50.
nerja@parador.es, www.parador.es.
Magnificent clifftop setting overlooking main beach. Gardens, pool.❁❁❁.
Marina Turquesa, Cártama, 2. Tel. 952 52 13 22.
info@marinaturquesa.com, www.marinaturquesa.com.
Immaculate, fully equipped apartments, one to three bedrooms, grouped around a lawn and swimming pool. Gym, sauna. ❁❁❁ (cheaper in winter months)
Mena, El Barrio, 15. Tel. 952 52 05 41. hostalmena@hotmail.com.
Basic old-style hostal. Budget.
Tres Soles, Hernando de Carabeo, 40. Tel. 952 52 51 57.
hostal3soles@terra.es, www.hostaltresoles.com.
Budget hostal overlooking sea.

PERIANA
Cortijo Las Monjas, Ctra Riogordo-Alfarnate. Tel. 952 53 65 13. lasmonjas@cortijolasmonjas.com, www.cortijolasmonjas.com.
Renovated three-centuries-old farmhouse in beautiful rural area. Six rooms. Kitchen.

RINCÓN DE LA VICTORIA
Rincón Sol, Avda del Mediterráneo, 174. Tel. 952 40 11 00.
rinconsol@spa.es, www.rinconsol.com.
Modern, four-star hotel on beach. Handy for Málaga.

TORRE DEL MAR
Miraya, Calle Patrón Veneno, 6, Paseo Marítimo. Tel. 952 54 59 69.
hotelmiraya@wanadoo.es, www.hotelmiraya.com. Small, modern seafront hotel. Comfortable rooms with satellite TV, hair dryers, airconditioning.

VÉLEZ-MÁLAGA
Cortijo Los Vargas, Ctra de Arenas, km1.5. Tel. 952 50 29 36.
cortijolosvargas@telefonica.net, www.costasolrural-cortijovargas.com.
Converted farmhouse, views towards Med. Pool.

VIÑUELA, LA
La Viñuela, Presa de la Viñuela (north from Vélez-Málaga on
A335 towards Alhama). Tel. 952 51 91 93.
hotelvinuela@inicia.es, www.hotelvinuela.com. Modern,
well-equipped hotel overlooking lake. Pool. Restaurant. ✤✤✤

CAMPING
(some camp sites also let bungalows)

ALMAYATE
Almayate-Costa, Ctra N340, km267. Tel. 952 55 62 89.
Almayate-Costa, Carril de la Torre, s/n. Tel. 952 55 64 62.
Naturist camp site.
COMARES
Mirador de la Axarquía, next to sportsground. Tel. 952 50 92 09.

IZNATE
Camping Rural, Ctra Cajiz-Iznate. Tel. 952 03 06 06.
www.campingiznate.com.

Nerja

NERJA
Nerja, Ctra N340, km.297.
Tel. 952 52 97 14. Near to
Maro.

TORRE DEL MAR
Torre del Mar, Paseo
Marítimo. Tel. 952 54 02
24.

VALLENIZA
Valleniza, Ctra N340,
km264. Tel. 952 51 31 81.
10km from
Rincón de la Victoria.

GRANADA PROVINCE ACCOMMODATION

ALMUÑÉCAR

Almuñécar Playa, Paseo de San Cristóbal, s/n. Tel. 958 63 94 50.
milia@almunecar@solmelia.com, www.solmelia.com.
Four-star accommodation with all facilities, on seafront. ✳✳✳
Casablanca, Plaza San Cristóbal, 4. Tel 958 63 55 75.
hotelcasablanca@terra.com.
Two stars. Moorish-style décor. Aircon. Close to El Peñón del
Santo and beach.
Goya, Avenida de Europa, 31. Tel: 958 63 11 92. Comfortable,
unpretentious one-star hotel a block or so from the beach.
Budget, except July-Sept.
Peña Escrita nature park. Tel. 615 32 14 62.
reservas@pescrita.com, www.pescrita.com.
14km from Almuñécar in a 500-hectare park high in Sierra
Almijara. One of Andalusia's most curious overnight spots.
Wooden cabins sleeping up to eight people. Also camping.

CARCHUNA

Perla de Andalucía, Carchuna, s/n. Tel. 958 62 41 22.
perla@eh.etursa.es, www.eh.etursa.es/perla.
Low-rise, three-star hotel next to the beach. Pool. Closed mid-Oct
to April.

HERRADURA, LA

Los Fenicios, Paseo Andrés Segovia, s/n. Tel. 958 82 79 00.
sol.los.fenicios@solmelia.com, www.solmelia.com.
Stylish, four-star hotel. On seafront. Pool. Airconditioned. ✳✳✳
La Tartana, Urb. San Nicolás, Ctra de Málaga, km308.
Tel: 958 64 05 35. reservations@hotellatartana.com,
www.hotellatartana.com.
Intimate, antique décor, sunny terraces. American-German
management. Restaurant (closed Sun, Nov-June also closed Mon)
serves "world fusion" cuisine (hamburgers to Thai green curry).
Peña Parda, Paseo Andrés Segovia, 65. Tel. 958 64 00 66.
Pleasant seafront pension. Restaurant. Budget (more for rooms
with terraces).

MAMOLA, LA

Pensión Amat, Paseo Marítimo, 32. Tel. 958 82 95 02.
Friendly sea-front pension. Shared bathroom. Budget.

Casa de los Bates, Motril

MOTRIL

Casa de los Bates, N340, km329.5. (Safest approach from Motril side.) Tel. 958 34 94 95. info@casadelosbates.com, www.casadelosbates.com.

Old-style luxury in 19th-century hilltop manor house amid tropical gardens (see Motril sights). Marble floors, antiques. Rooms named Eugenia, Habana, Hierbabuena, Eucalipto and Buganvilla. ✳✳✳

OTÍVAR

Palacete de Cázulas, Caserío de Cázulas. Tel. 958 64 40 36. info@cazulas.com, www.cazulas.com.

For those who can afford to pay for luxury and total privacy. Dating back to the 15th century, this mansion once belonged to an aristocratic family. Painstakingly restored by British owners. Set amid the hills above Otívar, it has its own chapel, tennis court, spring-fed pool and extensive gardens. The main house sleeps up to 20. Rent: from 8,800 euros a week. ✳✳✳

RÁBITA, LA

Las Conchas, Paseo Marítimo, 55. Tel. 958 82 90 17. hotellasconchas@granada.net, www.hotellasconchas.com.

In an area where there is little choice. One star, modern facilities, near the beach. Closed October-April.

SALOBREÑA
Hostal Jayma, Calle Cristo, 24. Tel. 958 61 02 31.
info@hostaljayma.com, www.hostaljayma.com.
Small hostal, modern installations.
Faldas del Castillo, Calle Faldas del Castillo, 15. Tel. 630 073 794.
faldasdelcastillo@hotmail.com, www.faldasdelcastillo.com.
Two refurbished houses high in town near the castle walls.

CAMPING

CASTELL DE FERRO
Huerta Romero, Paseo Marítimo, 18. Tel. 958 65 60 01.
huertaromero@cyberpyme-andalucia.com

CARCHUNA
Don Cáctus. Tel. 958 6231 09.
camping@doncactus.com, www.doncactus.com.

HERRADURA, LA
La Herradura, Paseo Andrés Segovia. Tel. 958 64 00 56.

MOTRIL
Playa de Poniente. Tel. 958 82 03 03.
camplapo@infonegocio.com, www.infonegocio.com/camplapo.

LECRÍN VALLEY ACCOMMODATION

CÓNCHAR
Las Albercas de Cónchar, Huertecilla, 7. Tel. 958 77 71 05.
reservas@albercasdeconchar.es, www.albercasdeconchar.es.
Small, intimate hotel amid olive and orange orchards. Pool, Internet
connection. Restaurant serving local dishes.

DÚRCAL
Mariami, Comandante Lázaro, 82. Tel. 958 78 09 11.
elgaleon@teleline.es, www.turinet/empresa/hotelmariami.
Modern two-star hotel near town centre. Its Galeón restaurant
offers traditional dishes.

MELEGÍS
Los Naranjos, Avda Del Valle, 32. Tel. 958 79 34 14.
Accommodation with mod cons next to a popular restaurant. Looks
out over orange groves. Budget.

NIGÜELAS
Alquería de los Lentos, Camino de los Molinos. Tel. 958 77 78 50.
info@loslentoshotel.com, www.loslentoshotel.com.
Rural hotel in converted 16th-century mill. Pool. Restaurant.

WHERE TO EAT

First, an *aperitivo* is in order. Why not a *palito de ron*? Originating in Motril, this drink is prepared with rum, sugar, cinnamon, lemon and orange peel. The rum should be a Ron Pálido. The sugar cane industry has died but a lone Motril producer continues distilling this worthy product.

Hundreds of eating places exist along the coast, offering cuisines ranging from traditional Spanish to Greek, Mexican, Indian and Thai. Inland the choice is sparser. However, in smaller villages there is usually a bar serving *raciones* (platefuls of fish or meat) and/or a selection of tapas.

Generally, the further away you get from the cosmopolitan coast the lower are the prices. "International cuisine" can be a pitfall, as it often means food intended to be acceptable to all tastes, i.e. bland and acceptable to nobody.

Trying local specialities is part of the adventure of travelling the interior. Every village prides itself on particular dishes made from fresh local products. They are usually tasty and very good value.

Look out for the *menú del día*. This is the set meal, three hearty courses with a glass of wine, costing seven euros or little more. If the restaurant is packed with local workers at 2pm, you can be assured you'll get a filling meal. There may be no written menu.

Ventas. These roadside inns offer a bargain-priced set lunch. They are usually cheap and cheerful with basic decor and the ubiquitous television blaring out information which nobody pays any attention to.

Chiringuitos. These are beach restaurants. Not so long ago they were merely shacks offering basic food, but now have been seriously upgraded. The food has become more varied and sophisticated and hygiene standards are much higher. No longer the bargain they once were, they usually specialise in fresh seafood.

Prices. In most of the restaurants recommended in this book, a three-course meal without wine costs from 20 to 35 euros per person. "Budget" means you can eat for less than 20 euros. The symbols *** indicate a meal will cost more than 35 euros. A 10 per cent tip is adequate, unless service is exceptional.

Plastic. Most places now accept Visa and MasterCard credit cards, less frequently Diners and American Express. At cheaper establishments, ventas and bars, it's cash on the nail.

Opening hours. Lunch is usually served between 1.30 and 3pm, dinner between 9 and 11pm, except in restaurants on the coast which cater to tourists and start serving an hour or so earlier. The simplest way for north Europeans to adjust their eating habits to Spanish ways is to add one to two hours to the times on their watches. Tapas are usually available at all hours. At popular spots on Sundays lunch can be served any time between 1 and 5pm.

Note: many restaurants in tourist zones close for holidays during January and early February.

Off limits. In some restaurants you may be offered *chanquetes*, a Málaga favourite. Resist the temptation. Catching this tiny fish has been banned because it is virtually fished out. As a result the baby offspring of other species may be offered as *"chanquetes"*, thus endangering their future too.

AXARQUÍA RESTAURANTS

ALFARNATE
Venta de Alfarnate, Antigua Ctra Málaga-Granada, km513.
Tel. 952 75 93 88. Closed Mon. Claimed to be Andalusia's oldest inn. Hearty grills and stews. Book at weekends.

Venta de Alfarnate

ÁRCHEZ

Posada Mudéjar, Álamo, 6. Tel. 952 55 31 06.
www.posadamesonmudejar.com.
Closed Wed. Cosy restaurant and inn in restored house. Andalusian
dishes. Won rural tourism prize as best *mesón*.
Venta El Curro, Ctra Corumbela s/n. Tel 678 618 119. Closed Tues.
Terrace. Tapas. Specialities barbecued pork, kid and lamb (order
in advance). Budget dish: Plato El Curro, eggs, sausage, black
pudding.

BENAJARAFE

Castillo del Marqués, Escuela de Hostelería, Ctra N340, s/n,
Valle-Niza (between Rincón and Torre del Mar).
Tel. 952 51 42 87. castillodelmarques@hotmail.com.
Only open Thursdays for lunch. Closed mid-June to end-October.
Unique setting in a fortress courtyard. Keen young catering
students cook and serve a set meal of traditional dishes at a bargain
price. Reserve at least one week in advance.

CANILLAS DE ALBAIDA

La Plaza, La Plaza. Tel. 952 55 32 54. Closed Wed. Next to
La Expectación church. Outside dining. Tapas and well-prepared
traditional dishes, such as roast kid, boar and partridge.

CANILLAS DE ACEITUNO

La Sociedad, Calle Iglesia, 12. Tel. 952 51 82 92. Closed Mon pm.
Friendly bar-restaurant. Local dishes include fennel soup, kid with
garlic, stewed rabbit. Budget.

COMARES

El Molino de los Abuelos, Plaza, 2. Tel. 952 50 93 09.
info@molino-abuelos.com www.molino-abuelos.com.
Rambling mansion with olive mill and bodega. Old beams, artefacts,
paintings and photos. Roast lamb and chicken rolls stuffed with shrimps.

CÓMPETA

Cortijo Paco, Avda Canillas, 6. Tel. 952 55 36 47.
www.cortijopaco.es. Closed Mon. June-Aug only open for dinner,
except weekends. Suckling pig, grilled salmon. Fine views.
Museo del Vino, Avda Constitución, Edif. Axarquía bajo.
Tel 952 55 33 14. Closed Mon. Large bar/restaurant decorated in
rustic style. Organic ham, ostrich fillet, grilled kid. Raisins, honey
on sale.

FRIGILIANA
Las Chinas, Plaza Doña Amparo Guerrero, 16. (Planning move to location adjoining Casco Viejo.) Tel. 952 53 41 35. Closed Tues. Good price-quality ratio, friendly professional service. Reservation advisable for dinner.
Taberna del Sacristán, Plaza de la Iglesia, 12. Tel. 952 53 30 09. www.latabernadelsacristan.com. Closed Tues. Excellent-quality traditional dishes with imaginative touches. Tables on the plaza.

NERJA
Casa Luque, Plaza Cavana, 2. Tel. 952 52 10 04. www.casaluque.com. Closed Wed & part Jan-Feb. Fine old house with terrace. Imaginative tapas. Traditional dishes, roast lamb with rosemary honey. ❋❋❋
Haveli, Calle Cristo, 42-44. Tel. 952 52 42 97. Evenings only, except Sun. Closed Mon in winter, summer open daily. Popular Indian restaurant, one of the first on the coast.
Lan Sang, Málaga, 12, Edif. Cuatro Caminos. Tel. 952 52 80 53. www.lansang.com. Closed Sun lunch, Mon. Tasty Laotian and Thai cuisine. Friendly service. Budget set lunch.
Mesón Antonio, Diputación Provincial, 18. Tel. 952 52 00 33. Closed Wed. Congenial spot with traditional Spanish dishes. Good tapas at the bar.

PERIANA
Café-Bar Verdugo, Plaza Bellavista. Tel. 952 53 60 69. Closed Wed pm. Hearty, no frills fare. Budget set meal.

RINCÓN DE LA VICTORIA
Mulse, Calle del Túnel, 10. (Málaga end of Paseo Marítimo near tunnel.) Tel. 952 40 13 65. www.mulse.es. Closed Sun & Mon. Seafront restaurant with elegant, Danish-style décor. Imaginative Spanish-international cuisine (wild boar croquettes, crepes stuffed with ham). Live music, jazz, flamenco, rock, in ground-floor bar Fridays.

RIOGORDO
Magiaza, Camino Magiaza, 24. Tel. 952 73 25 89. Winter months open only Fri, Sat, Sun, holidays. Summer, open Tues-Sun. Home cooking. Grilled meat, suckling pig.

SEDELLA
Lorena, Villa del Castillo, 20. Tel. 952 50 88 50. Specialities include

paella (call two hours in advance), *chivo en salsa* (kid in sauce) and *cochinillo al horno* (roast suckling pig*)*.

TORRE DEL MAR
Fernando, Calle del Mar, 71. Tel. 952 54 21 74. Closed Thurs.
Good-priced seafood. Bar and terrace.
La Cueva, Paseo de Larios, 12.
Tel. (reservations restaurant) 952 54 40 34. One of the town's most popular spots for eating excellent fresh seafood.
El Radar, Paseo Marítimo, 13. Tel. 952 54 10 82. Closed Wed.
Seafront location, reasonably priced seafood.
Italia, Avda Toré Toré, Edif. Hamburgo, 1. Tel. 952 54 04 48.
www.pizzeriaitalia.org. Closed Mon. Well-prepared Italian dishes.
Budget.

TORROX-COSTA
El Quinto Pino, Bloque 6, Costa del Oro. Tel. 952 53 47 59.
Evenings only. Closed Mon. German-run. Creative international dishes. Try tomato soup with gin and cream, or baked strawberries stuffed with marzipan, ice cream and cream. ❉ ❉

GRANADA PROVINCE RESTAURANTS

ALMUÑÉCAR
Pepe Dígame, Paseo de las Flores, Playa de San Cristóbal.
Tel. 958 34 93 15. Relaxed beach restaurant. Seafood specialities.
Budget-priced set lunch.
Los Geranios, Plaza de la Rosa, 4. Tel. 958 63 40 20.
Closed Sun pm and Mon. Cosy spot. Specialities from Andalusian provinces, including *costillas en adobo* (Granada) and eggs, chops and *patatas a lo pobre* (Almuñécar).

Almuñécar by night

Horno de Cándida, Orovia, 3. Tel. 958 88 32 84. Located in a former bakery. Ancient well at the entrance, one dining room in the vaulted oven. Traditional Andalusian dishes with modern touches. Venison stew, Mozarab-style lamb with fried chickpeas. Gastronomic menu.

Jacquy Cotobro, Edificio Río, Playa Cotobro. Tel: 958 63 18 02. Closed Monday. French-style cuisine delightfully presented. Some of the best food on the coast. With a gastronomic menu. ***

Mar de Plata, Playa San Cristóbal, Edif. Mar de Plata. Tel. 958 63 30 79. Closed Tues. Excellent seafood, home-made desserts.

Mesón Gala, Plaza Damasco, 5. Tel. 958 88 14 55. Closed Wed. On a small square honouring playwright Antonio Gala. Chickpeas with lobster, pork dishes, tapas. Budget set meal.

La Última Ola, Puerta del Mar, 4-5. Tel. 958 63 00 18. Closed: Mon & six weeks in winter. On the seafront. Seafood, paella. Budget menu.

GUÁJAR ALTO
Carmen, Carretera, 8. Tel. 958 62 00 06. Carmen serves vast portions of home-cooked kid in almond sauce, rabbit, pork, chicken. Budget.

HERRADURA, LA
Mesón El Tinao, Paseo Andrés Segovia. Tel. 958 82 74 88. Closed Wed. Popular restaurant serving traditional dishes with imaginative touches. Paella, lamb chops, duck breast with mango and vanilla.

MOTRIL
Tropical, Avda Rodríguez Acosta, 23. Tel. 958 60 04 50. Location, in a modern building next to a petrol station, is not promising. But the Tropical is highly rated by locals. Seafood, grilled meats. ***

MURTAS
Mesón Cuatro Vientos, Carretera de Murtas, km4. Tel. 630 236 244. Part of the adjoining winery (see Contraviesa's new image). Rustic architecture. Excellent charcoal-grilled kid, lamb and pork. Budget menu. Views of the Sierra Nevada.

OTÍVAR
El Capricho, Carretera, s/n. Tel. 958 64 50 75. Closed Mon. www.rebalae.com/elcapricho. Chicken with apple is the speciality, also roast lamb (booked ahead). Terrace. Can get crowded. Budget.

SALOBREÑA
El Peñon, Playa del Peñon. Tel. 958 61 05 38.
www.restauranteelpenon.com, info@restauranteelpenon.com.
Closed Mon & mid-Jan to mid-Feb. Perched on a rock. Excellent
seafood, service. Good-value special menu.
Pesetas, Calle Bóveda, 11. Tel 958 61 01 82. Closed Mon.
Near castle walls in old quarter. Magnificent view from terrace.
Humble bar expanded into restaurant with not-quite-so-humble
prices for seafood.

LECRÍN VALLEY

Popular local dishes in the valley include fennel stew, *remojón de naranja*
(orange and cod salad) and *pisto de calabaza* (pumpkin ratatouille) and
snails in sauce.

DÚRCAL
El Molino de Dúrcal, Puente de Dúrcal, s/n. Tel. 958 78 07 31.
biodurc@teleline.es, www.elmolinodelpuente.com. Closed Mon.
Converted mill, also offering accommodation. Imaginative dishes.

MELEGÍS
Los Naranjos, Avda Del Valle, 32. Tel. 958 79 34 14. Closed Wed.
Specialities, kid and paella. Budget menu. Sunny terrace.

RESTÁBAL
Bar Jovi/Mesón Despensa Del Valle, Santa Ana, 5.
Tel. 958 793 598/531. Closed Tues. Tapas in Bar Jovi, excellent
meals in the restaurant. Grilled lamb chops, fennel stew

DRIVING

Spain has taken stern measures in a bid to reduce the mortality rate on its
roads. On-the-spot fines are heavy and a points system operates, whereby
accumulated infractions result in automatic loss of licence. The best advice:
be extra cautious.

Driving is on the right and traffic entering from the right has priority
unless otherwise signalled. Be wary on country routes, as vehicles may
come around on bends in the centre of the road. Drivers and passengers
must use seat belts.

Road signs are sometimes over-optimistic, encouraging you to overtake
when it is decidedly risky. Or they can be misleading. "Road closed"

Sierra road to Granada

usually means that, but it could be that the road was under repair two years earlier and nobody bothered to remove the sign.

Motorcycles without lights, mules and other livestock can be hazards at night. Motor-cyclists must wear crash helmets, although teenage riders often ignore this law and others, e.g. trying to overtake on the inside.

The speed limit in urban areas is usually 30mph (50kph). On main roads the limit is usually 50mph (80km) to 62mph (100kph). On autoroutes the limit is 75mph (120km).

Petrol stations are much more numerous than a few years ago, but can be sparse in country areas where they usually close at night. Prices vary little although gas stations at hypermarkets are often cheaper. Leadless petrol is widely available, Euro super (95 octane) and Super plus (98 octane).

If driving your own vehicle, bring the car documents, international insurance and a bail bond in case of accident, an international driving licence (although for short stays by EEC visitors your national licence should be sufficient), spare car light bulbs, fanbelt and a red warning triangle. By law you must carry a reflective jacket to wear at night if you have to get out of the vehicle on a highway.

ESSENTIAL MAPS

Michelin's map of Andalusia (no. 446, scale 1:400,000) is recommended. The annual Campsa guide has fold-out maps of all Spain, plus tourist and gastronomic information.

Hikers should obtain the Mapas Topográficos of Sierra Tejeda and Sierra Almijara, designed by Miguel Angel Torres Delgado. This covers the nature park on a scale of 1:25,000.

Sierra del Jobo

LOMA DE LA BADANA

Sierra de

888
Alfarnate
R

859
Alfarnatejo
R

Sierra de Camorolos

Los Baños de Vilo   Marchamona

Masada del Moro

Sabar
150 m.

Gonzalo

Mondrón

ctra. del arco

Cortijo Blanco

547
Periana
R

Toril

Los Marines

405
Riogordo
R

Despoblado medieval
de las Mesas de Zalia

Pilarero

694
Colmenar
R

El Cerro

Pinturas rupestres de
las Piedras de Cabrera

Caravaca

Puente de Zalia

Los Cortijuelos

Solano

Ermita del Espejo

Río

Los Rozas

Los Casillas

Embalse
de la
Viñuela

151
Viñue
R

Las Cuevas Romo

Cueva

Los Romanes

Los Gómez
La Alde

Las F

933

La Zubia

Las Umbrías

Los Gómez

Portugalejo

Ermita del Cerro del Moro

Comares
R
720

Salto del Negro

Masmúllar

96
Benamargosa
R

733

Cútar
337

Triana

ontes de   Málaga

Los Ventorros

544

237
El Borge
R

Alcoscolar

Puerto
del León

Santa Pitar

La Sern

229
Almáchar
R

Río Almáchar

126
Benamocarra
H R

**Parque Natural
de los
Montes de Málaga**

Venta de Cárdenas

Santonina

Aerodromo

Límite Axarquía

1190

Vallejo

451
Moclinejo
R

311
Iznate
R

Cabrillas

513

Santa Catalina

Cerrado de
Calderón

397
Totalán
R

Valdés

235
Macharaviaya
R

Benaque
R

Cajíz
R

El Capitán

Almayate Alt

Olías

512

Despoblado
Medieval
de Miximbiana

Benalgalbón

Almayate B.

Chilches
R

Colina
Soleada

ctra. del arco

Playa
de
la Caleta

El Palo

Torre del Tesoro
Parque Arqueológico

Añoreta Golf

La Sirena
R

140

Torre del Jaral

Torre Paloma

**La Cala
del Moral**

Torre de Cantal

Torre de R

**Rincón de
la Victoria**

**Torre de
Benagalbón**

Torre de Chilches

Benajarafe

Torre Moya

Playa Baja Mar

Ensenada de Málaga

MÁLAGA

uerto a 20 minutos
Axarquía (Costa del Sol)

Playa Cala del Moral   Playa Rincón de la Victoria   Playa de Benagalbón   Playa Los Rubios   Playa de Chilches   Playa de Benajarafe   Playa Valle Niza

AXARQUÍA
COSTA DEL SOL

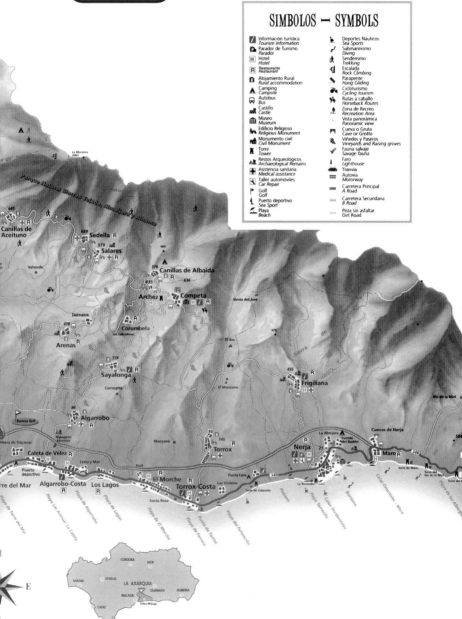

SIMBOLOS — SYMBOLS

- Información turística / *Tourism information*
- Parador de Turismo / *Parador*
- Hotel / *Hotel*
- Restaurante / *Restaurant*
- Alojamiento Rural / *Rural accommodation*
- Camping / *Campsite*
- Autobus / *Bus*
- Castillo / *Castle*
- Museo / *Museum*
- Edificio Religioso / *Religious Monument*
- Monumento civil / *Civil Monument*
- Torre / *Tower*
- Restos Arqueológicos / *Archaeological Remains*
- Asistencia sanitaria / *Medical assistance*
- Taller automóviles / *Car Repair*
- Golf / *Golf*
- Puerto deportivo / *Sea Sport*
- Playa / *Beach*

- Deportes Náuticos / *Sea Sports*
- Submarinismo / *Diving*
- Senderismo / *Trekking*
- Escalada / *Rock Climbing*
- Parapente / *Hang Gliding*
- Cicloturismo / *Cycling tourism*
- Rutas a caballo / *Horseback Routes*
- Zona de Recreo / *Recreation Area*
- Vista panorámica / *Panoramic view*
- Cueva o Gruta / *Cave or Grotto*
- Viñedos y Paseros / *Vineyards and Raising groves*
- Fauna salvaje / *Savage fauna*
- Faro / *Lighthouse*
- Tranvia / *Tramway*
- Autovia / *Motorway*
- Carretera Principal / *A Road*
- Carretera Secundaria / *B Road*
- Pista sin asfaltar / *Dirt Road*

157

Sierra del Chaparral

Guájar
Faragüit

Lentejí

Guájar Fondón

Vélez
de Benaudall

Otivar

Itrabo

Río Guadalfeo

La Gelibra

Jete

La Gorgarach

Río Verde

Lobres

Los Tab

El Cerval

Molvízar

Los Guerras

El Saucillo

Salobreña

Motril

Torrecuevas

La Caleta

La Herradura

Almuñecar

MÁLAGA

Pun

Torrenu

MEDITERRANEAN
COSTA

Torvizcón
Alcázar
Contraviesa
Fregenite
Bargís
El C
Olías
Haza del Lino
Albondón
Alfornón
Los Gálvez
Rubite
Polopos
Lújar
Casafuer
Sorvilán
Albuñol
Haza
Jolujar
Los Yesos   Melicena
El P
Gualchos   Castillo de Baños
a Garnatilla
La Mamola
La Rábita

ALMERÍA

Castell de Ferro

Calahonda
chuna

S E A

T R O P I C A L

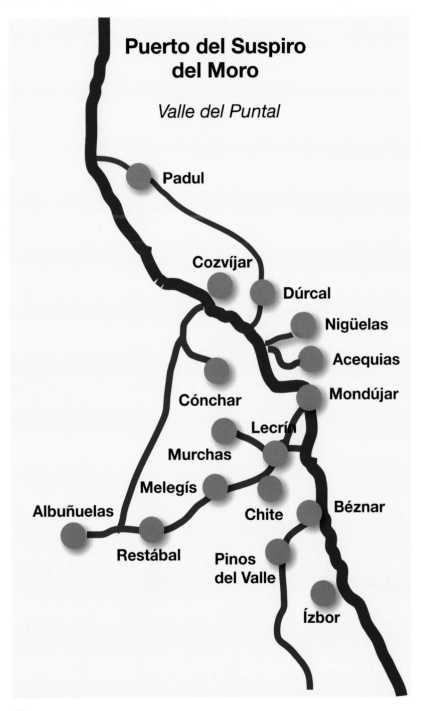

Puerto del Suspiro del Moro

Valle del Puntal

Padul

Cozvíjar

Dúrcal

Nigüelas

Acequias

Cónchar

Mondújar

Lecrín

Murchas

Melegís

Chite

Béznar

Albuñuelas

Restábal

Pinos del Valle

Ízbor

SPORTING ACTIVITIES

DIVING

ALMUÑÉCAR

Almuñécar Dive Centre, Paseo Cotobro, 6. Tel. 958 63 45 12.
Scuba Océano, Paseo de Cotobro, Edif. Delfín, Local 10.
Tel 958 63 21 25.
scubaoceano@telefonica.net, www.scubaoceano.com.

CALAHONDA

Escuela de Buceo Dardanus, Fragata Cervantes s/n.
Tel. 958 62 40 66/699 094 550. www.buceodardanus.com
Courses at all levels, Scuba Schools International diplomas.
Nitrox.

HERRADURA, LA

Cabosur Buceo, Paseo Andrés Segovia, s/n, near Nuevo
Camping. Tel. 958 82 73 77. cabosurbuceol@cobasurbuceo.com
www.cabosurbuceo.com.
Granada Sub. Tel. 958 64 02 81. luismi@granadasub.com
www.granadasub.com.
Marazul Buceo, Urb. Rosa Náutica, s/n. Tel. 958 64 01 18.
marazul@marazulbuceo.com, www.marazulbuceo.com

MARINA DEL ESTE

Buceo La Herradura, Tel. 958 82 70 83.
info@buceolaherradura.com www.buceolaherradura.com.
PADI courses. Nitrox, rebreather.
Club Nautique. Tel. 958 82 75 14.
dive@clubnautique.com www.clubnautique.com

MORCHE, EL

Scubadoo, Paseo Marítimo, 22. Tel. 952 96 71 26.
dive@scubadoospain.com. PADI dive centre. Underwater scooters.

NERJA

Buceo Costa Nerja, Playa Burriana. Tel. 952 52 86 10.
mail@nerjadiving.com, www.nerjadiving.com. PADI courses.
Club Nautique, Avda Castilla Pérez, 2. Tel. 952 52 46 54.
Diving school. Outdoor activities.

TORRE DEL MAR
Apañao Sub, Conjunto El Copo (local 11). Tel. 952 54 02 91.
Specialised shop and info for skin-divers.

HORSE RIDING
(trekking, lessons)

ALCAUCÍN
Horseshoe Ranch. Tel. 620 609 374. charlygalvin@yahoo.co.uk.

ALMUÑÉCAR
Centro Ecuestre Tropical, Barranco Caballero, s/n.
Tel. 609 568 966. www.almunecar.info/ecuestre.
Fully equipped municipal centre. Classes, dressage, horse training,
mountain and beach rides.

CÓMPETA
Los Caballos del Mosquín. Tel. 608 658 108.
caballosmosquin@hotmail.com, www.horseriding-andalucia.com.

SALOBREÑA
Rock Beach Ranch (below Hotel Salobreña). Tel. 664 016 069.
rockbeachranch@hotmail.com.

GO-KARTING

Karting del Sol, Torre del Mar (on N340 towards Almayate).
Tel. 686 970 365. Two circuits, one for children, 20 karts.

ADVENTURE, PARAGLIDING

ALMUÑÉCAR
Club de Vuelo Fly Park, Urbanización La Ribera. Tel. 666 816 381.
info@fly-park-almunecar.com, www.fly-park-almunecar.com.
Paragliding and hang-gliding courses.
Zate Aventuras, Avda Costa del Sol, 31 – 9. Tel. 958 12 14 72.
zate@telefonica.net. Qualified instructors. Rock climbing,
trekking.

CALAHONDA
Tropiactivo, Camping Don Cactus. Tel. 958 62 31 09.
info@tropiactivo.com www.tropiactivo.com
Rock-climbing, hiking, paintball, canyoning, diving, windsurfing.

Calahorra

Wingbeat. Tel. 697 272 957. wingbeatspain@hotmail.com Hiking, biking, snowboards, quads, bird-watching. Three languages.

NERJA

Life Adventure, Antonio Ferrándis, 39. 677 894 002. info@lifeadventure.es, www.lifeadventure.es. Jeep tours, mountainbiking.
Nerja Adventures S.L., Hostal San Miguel, San Miguel, 36. Tel. 952 52 18 86. www.nerjaadventures.com info@nerjaadventures.com. Canyoning, diving, kite boarding, jeep safaris.

WATER PARKS

ALMUÑÉCAR
Aquatropic, Playa de la Velilla. Tel. 958 63 33 16. info@aqua-tropic.com, www.aqua-tropic.com. Open June-September. Kamikaze, children's pool, disco.

TORRE DEL MAR
Aquavelis, Urb. El Tomillar. Tel. 952 54 27 58. aquavelis@telefonica.net, www.aquavelis.com. Kamikazes, waterfalls, café. Open June-September.

BOATING, WINDSURF

ALMUÑÉCAR
Alquiler de Barcos, Playa Fuente Piedra (ext to breakwater).
Tel. 617 683 344. www.alquilerbarcosct.com. Excursions and rental
of motor craft.

CALAHONDA
Viento y Mar, Margarita, 2. Tel. 958 62 32 94.
info@vientoymar, www.vientoymar.com. Sailboat rental.

HERRADURA, LA
Windsurf La Herradura, Paseo Marítimo, 34. Tel. 958 64 01 43.
info@windsurflaherradura.com, www.windsurflaherradura.com.
Sailboats, cats, windsurf, canoes.

GOLF
Five courses are within easy reach, two in the Axarquía, one on the Costa
Tropical, one near Granada and one in Málaga's eastern suburb of El
Candado. The Federación Andaluza de Golf publishes an annual guide
with details of all courses and competition dates. The Federation's official
website is www.fga.org.

El Candado, Urb. El Candado, Málaga. Tel. 952 29 93 40.
candado@golf-andalucia.net. Small, nine-hole course on various
levels. Short but complex. Par: 64. Designed by Fernández Caleya.

Añoreta Golf, Urb. Añoreta Golf, Rincón de la Victoria (Málaga).
Tel. 952 40 40 00. www.anoretagolf.es, anoreta@golf-andalucia.net.
18 holes. Par: 72. Water hazards. Designed by José María Cañizares, it opened in 1990. Golf school with instruction in Spanish,
English and German. Off the A-7 autoroute, Macharaviaya exit.

Baviera Golf, 18 holes, Urb. Baviera Golf, Caleta de
Vélez (Málaga). Tel. 952 55 50 15. www.bavieragolf.com,
info@bavieragolf.com. 18 holes. Par: 71. Designed by José María
Cañizares. Wide fairways, suits all players, water obstacles.
Exit 272 on autoroute coming from Málaga.

Los Moriscos, Urb. Playa Grande, Motril (Granada). Tel. 958 82
55 27. moriscos@golf-andalucia.net. A fairly flat course, designed
by Ibergolf and Manuel Pinero. Generous greens, many lakes.
In sport and leisure complex near beach. Par: 72.

Granada Club de Golf, Avda de los Cosarios, s/n, Las Gabias
(Granada). Tel. 958 58 40 60. granada@golf-andalucia.net.
8km from Granada, 30km from the Costa Tropical. 18 holes.
Par: 71. Magnificent views of the Sierra Nevada. Clubs for rent.
Driving range.

MARINAS

Club Náutico Deportivo de Motril. 168 moorings. Tel. 958 60 00 37.
Caleta de Vélez. Tel. 952 5113 90. 236 moorings, up to 20 metres,
all available for rent.
El Candado, Málaga. Tel. 952 29 60 97. 215 moorings, all available
for rent.
Marina del Este, Punta de la Mona, La Herradura.
Tel. 958 64 08 01. marinaeste@marinasmediterraneo.com,
www.marinamediterraneos.com. Boats up to 30 metres, 227
moorings, 25 per cent available for rent. Crane for up to 30 tonnes.

BACKGROUND READING

Allan, Ted & Sydney Gordon: **The scalpel, the sword -
The story of Dr Norman Bethune** (McClelland & Stewart,
Toronto, 1989). Civil War and flight from Málaga to Almería.
Baird, David: **Sunny Side Up - The 20th century hits a Spanish
village** (Santana Books), changing times in an Axarquía community.
Brenan, Gerald: **South from Granada** (Penguin). Classic account
of life in a Granada village.
Caro Baroja, Julio: **Los Moriscos del Reino de Granada**
(Istmo, Madrid), the Moriscos and their rebellion.
Lee, Laurie: **As I Walked Out One Midsummer Morning**
(Penguin), poetic view of Spain as Civil War threatened; **A Rose
for Winter** (Penguin), Lee's return to post-Civil War Andalusia.
Montoro Fernández, Francisco: **Bandoleros de la Axarquía**
(Acento Andaluz, Málaga). Banditry in the 19th century.

HIKING GUIDES

Exploring the Axarquía by Elma Thompson. Indefatigable Elma
pioneered guided walks in this area and has produced a series of
invaluable leaflets.
Costa del Sol Walks, by Charles Davis (Santana Books).
From Nerja to Manilva.
Walking in Andalucía by Guy Hunter-Watts (Santana Books).
Walk! the Axarquía by Charles Davis (Discovery Walking
Guides). Includes GPS coordinates.
Andar por La Axarquía by Francisco José Guerrero Ruiz and
Alicia Franco Álvarez (Penthalón).
Caminando por el Parque Natural de las Sierras Almijara y Tejeda
by Jesús Cuartero Zueco and Cayetano Casado Bolívar (Arguval).

ENGLISH BOOKSHOPS

ALMUÑÉCAR
Delfin Books, Juan Carlos 1, 28. Tel. 958 634 120.
delfinbooks@kasbach28.com. English, German, Scandinavian
books. New and secondhand.

CÓMPETA
Todo Papel, Avda de la Constitución, 31. Tel. 952 55 37 55.
English, Spanish, German titles, newspapers.

DÚRCAL
Chris's Books, Pérez Carrillo, 32. Tel. 610 614 972.
caelliott2003@yahoo.co.uk. New and used books, cards.

NERJA
Smiffs, Almirante Ferrandiz, 10. Tel. 952 52 31 02.
info@booksaboutspain.com, www.booksaboutspain.com.
Wide selection, especially about Spain, hiking guides, cards.
Secondhand Book Centre, Granada, 32. Tel. 952 52 09 08.
Secondhand books in various languages.

TORRE DEL MAR
Pasatiempo, Calle Infantes, 30. Tel. 952 54 37 03.
bookshop@centerboot.com, www.bookshoppasatiempo.com.
English, German, French books.

VÉLEZ-MÁLAGA
Bookworld, Centro Comercial El Ingenio, Planta Baja 16,
Avda Juan Carlos1. Tel. 952 96 59 07.
elingenio@bookworldespana.com. Latest bestsellers, wide selection.

OPENING HOURS

Banks normally open between 8.30am and 2pm or 2.30pm, Mondays
to Fridays. They close earlier in summer. Some are open Saturday
mornings. Most shops open 10am-2pm, 5-9pm Mon-Sat. Shopping
malls are usually open 10am-10pm Mon-Sat. Monuments and
museums usually close on Mondays. However, those controlled
by local authorities may have different closing days — inquire at
tourism offices or town halls about opening times and access to
churches. Spain uses the 24-hour clock, so 10am-2pm is 10.00-14.00.
It is one hour ahead of British time, except briefly when the hour is
changed in spring and autumn.

STREET MARKETS

SUNDAY
Iznate
Nerja (car boot sale)

MONDAY:
Nigüelas
Torrox-Costa
Torrox
Vélez de Benaudalla

TUESDAY:
Benamocarra
Motril
Nerja
Salobrena

WEDNESDAY:
Algarrobo-Costa
Benamargosa
Dúrcal
Periana
Rincón de la Victoria

THURSDAY:
Albuñuelas
Cútar
Frigiliana
Torre del Mar
Vélez-Málaga

FRIDAY:
Almáchar
Almuñécar
Cala del Moral
La Herradura
Motril
Mondújar
Padul
Salobreña

SATURDAY:
Alcaucín
Almuñécar (car boot sale,
first Sat in month)
Caleta de Vélez
Comares
Cómpeta

SECURITY

Country areas such as the Axarquía and inland Granada are much safer than cities. Even so, commonsense precautions should be observed. Remember: hire cars are obvious targets because they may be carrying valuable possessions. Never leave valuables or documents in an unattended car at any time. Leave valuables, your passport and other documents in the hotel safe. Make photocopies if you want to carry identification.

When staying overnight, take all baggage into the hotel. If possible, in cities park your car in a garage or a guarded car-park. Unofficial parking attendants — dubbed "gorillas" by the locals — may ask you for money. The safest course is to give them something.

There are three distinct police forces:

"Los municipales" (blue uniforms, peaked caps) are employed by the local council for minor tasks such as bill collection and controlling traffic.

Civil Guards (olive-green uniforms, their distinctive patent leather tricorn hats have been relegated to ceremonial occasions) control small towns and rural areas. They also patrol the highways.

The National Police (dark blue uniforms), based in larger towns, are concerned with crime prevention and investigation. Police stations (*comisarías*) in tourist areas generally have report forms in several languages.

CONSULATES
(in Málaga unless otherwise stated)

Austria, Alameda de Colón, 26. Tel. 952 60 02 67
Belgium, Compositor Lehmberg Ruiz, 5. Tel. 952 23 99 07
Canada, Plaza de la Malagueta, 2, Edif Horizonte. 952 22 33 46
Denmark, Córdoba, 6. Tel. 952 21 17 97.
Finland, Blasco de Garay, 7. Tel. 952 21 24 35
France, Duquesa de Parcent, 8. Tel. 952 22 65 90
Germany, Mauricio M. Pareto, 2. Tel. 952 36 35 91
Great Britain, Mauricio M. Pareto, 2. Tel. 952 35 23 00
Ireland, Avda Los Boliches, 15, Fuengirola. Tel. 952 47 51 08
    Italy, Palestina, 3. Tel. 952 30 61 50
    Netherlands, Avda C. Alessandri, 33, Torremolinos. Tel. 952 38 08 88.
    Norway, Blasco de Garay, 7. Tel. 952 21 03 31
    Portugal, Cañizares, 15. Tel. 952 31 12 53
    Sweden, Córdoba, 6. 952 60 43 83.
    Switzerland, Alameda de Colón, 26. Tel. 952 21 72 66
    United States, Avda Juan Gómez Juanito, 8, Edif Lucía. Tel. 952 47 48 91

USEFUL PHONE NUMBERS, WEBSITES

AIRPORTS
Granada. Tel. 958 24 52 00
Málaga. Tel. 952 04 88 04 www.aena.es, www.iberia.com.

RAILWAY STATIONS
Granada, Avda de Andaluces. Tel. 958 27 12 72.
Málaga, Explanada de la Estación. Tel. 902 24 02 02. www.renfe.es

BUS STATIONS
Almuñécar. Tel. 958 63 01 40
Granada. Tel. 958 18 54 80
Málaga. Tel. 952 34 17 38
Motril. Tel. 958 60 00 64
Nerja. Tel. 952 52 15 04
Salobreña. Tel. 958 61 25 21
Torre del Mar. Tel. 952 54 09 36
Vélez-Málaga. Tel. 952 50 17 31

EMERGENCIES
All services 112
Ambulance 061
Civil Guard 062
National police 091
Red Cross 902 22 22 92

FIRE BRIGADE
Rincón de la Victoria. 952 40 20 57
Vélez-Málaga. 952 55 80 91

The Asociación para la Promoción Turística de la Axarquía (APTA), at Avda de Andalucía, 110, Torre del Mar (tel. 952 542 808) promotes the **Axarquía**. Its website is www.axarquiacostadelsol.es, email info@axarquiacostadelsol.es.

Granada's Patronato de Turismo promotes **the Costa Tropical**. Address: Plaza Mariana Pineda, 10-2nd floor, 18009 Granada. Tel 958 247 146. turismo@dipgra.es, www.turismodegranada.org, www.turgranada.com.

The **Junta de Andalucía** website has useful tourism information, www.andalucia.org. It can be contacted at info@andalucia.org and 901 20 00 20.

LEARNING THE LANGUAGE

It is possible to get by on the coast without knowing a word of Spanish. But that cuts you off from half the fun of visiting a foreign land. No matter how many mistakes you make, if you try to speak the language it will be appreciated. Bring a phrase book and a dictionary. Numerous language schools offer courses at all levels to those wishing to learn Spanish. Popular centres are Nerja, Almuñécar and Salobreña.

VOCABULARY

Emergencies
I am lost: *Estoy perdido*
There's been an accident: *Ha ocurrido un accidente*
I have been robbed: *He sido robado* or *me han robado*
Call the police: *Llama a la policía*
I have lost my passport, the car keys: *He perdido mi pasaporte, las llaves del coche*
I need a doctor: *Necesito un médico*
Ambulance: *ambulancia*
First aid post: *casa de socorro, puesto de socorro*
Police station: *comisaría de policía*
Red Cross: *Cruz Roja*
Civil Guard post: *cuartel de la Guardia Civil:*
Chemist, pharmacy: *farmacia*
Hospital: *hospital, sanitario*
Doctor: *médico*
Casualty department: *urgencias*

Useful basics
Please: *Por favor*
Thank you: *Gracias*
Good morning: *Buenos días*
Good afternoon: *Buenas tardes*
Good night: *Buenas noches*
Goodbye: *Adiós* or *Hasta luego*
Where is the post office, railway station, police station?:
Dónde está la oficina de correos, la estación de ferrocarril, la comisaría?

Where is the toilet?: *¿Dónde están los servicios (also "caballeros" and "damas")?*
Do you have a room free?: *¿Hay una habitación libre?*
How much is it?: *¿Cuánto es?*
Can I see the menu?: *¿Puedo ver la carta?*
The bill, please: *La cuenta, por favor*
What time is it?: *¿Qué hora es?*

Commonly used Spanish words

abierto: open
aficionado: amateur, fan (sport)
autobús or *autocar* (long distance): bus
ayer: yesterday
ayuntamiento, casa consistorial: town hall
barrio: quarter (of a city)
bodega: wine cellar
calle: street
cama: bed
cambiar: to change
campo: countryside, field
carretera: highway
cerrado: closed
cerveza: beer
ciudad: city
coche: car
comida: meal
corrida: bullfight
cortijo: farmhouse
dinero: money
finca: farm
fino: dry sherry
gitano: gypsy
hoy: today
jamón serrano: mountain-cured ham
mañana: tomorrow
mañana por la mañana: tomorrow morning
menú del día: set meal
mercado: market
mesón: bar-restaurant
mirador: viewpoint
moto: motor-cycle
pan: bread

parador: state-run hotel
playa: beach
plaza: square
pueblo: village, town
tablao: flamenco night club
tapa: snack
venta: inn

On the road
Is there a petrol station near here?:
¿Hay una gasolinera (or estación de servicio) por aquí?
Fill her up, please: *Lleno, por favor*
Where is the road to Torrox?:
¿Dónde está la carretera para Torrox?
How do I get to the airport, the market?:
¿Como se puede ir al aeropuerto, al mercado?
crossroads: *cruce*
traffic lights: *semáforos*
driving licence: *carnet de conducir*
insurance certificate: *certificado de seguro*

Road signs
Aparcamiento: parking
Autovía: four-lane highway
Carga o descarga: Loading and unloading zone, no parking
Carretera cortada: road blocked
Ceda el paso: give way
Centro urbano: town centre
Circunvalación, ronda: bypass
Entrada: entrance
Llamamos grúa: We call the tow-truck (i.e. no parking)
Prohibido aparcar, no aparcar: parking forbidden
Prohibido el paso: no entry
Salida: exit
Tramo en obras: road works
Vía única: one way

Architecture
alcazaba: castle
alcázar: fortress, royal palace
artesonado: Moorish-style coffered ceiling
azulejo: glazed tile
barroco: baroque, ornate style

capilla mayor: chapel with high altar
claustro: cloister
churrigueresco: Churrigueresque, highly ornate baroque art
coro: chancel with choir-stalls
ermita: hermitage
isabelino: Isabelline, Gothic style from era of Queen Isabel
mihrab: prayer niche in a mosque
mozárabe: Mozarab, art developed by Christians under Muslim rule
mudéjar: Muslim art in Christian-occupied territory
murallas: walls, ramparts
neo-clásico: neo-classical, imitating sober Greek and Roman styles
plateresco: Plateresque, finely carved early Renaissance style
qibla: mosque wall orientated towards Mecca
reja: iron grille
retablo: decorated altarpiece
torre del homenaje: keep

INDEX